THE STORY OF THE BIBLE

the way Jesus and the apostles told it

by
Dr Richard Bustraan

D1265196

a2zBible *Publications* • Charlotte, North Carolina

THE STORY OF THE BIBLE
the way Jesus and the apostles told it

a2zBible *Publications*
Charlotte, North Carolina

www.a2zBible.com

ISBN 13: 978-0-9979534-0-4

Cataloguing–in–Publication data:

Bustraan, Richard A.

    The Story of the Bible : the way Jesus and the apostles told it /
Richard A. Bustraan.

      iii + 140 pp. ; 23cm.

      ISBN 13: 978-0-9979534-0-4

    1. The Bible—Works About the Bible—Criticism/Interpretation. I.
Title

BS500–534.8 2016

to God my Savior, who alone is wise

with tender devotion, to my earthly treasure, my Khasi princess

with affection and gratitude to my loving Mom

CONTENTS

Maps, Timelines, Charts

PREFACE

The premise of this book is simple. The Bible tells a story. From the first book, Genesis, to the last book, Revelation, God tells a story that begins with creation and extends into eternity. According to Jesus, the story can be summarized in three prophecies. In this book, I will show you that Jesus taught the apostles how to sum up the Bible in three prophecies and that they taught their followers the same message. Then, we will walk through the entire Bible to trace the development of these prophecies. If you understand these three prophecies, you will understand the story of the Bible the way Jesus and the apostles told it.

The Story of the Bible is perhaps the most life changing Bible study that I have ever taught and many have expressed to me that it has altered the way they see the Bible and their purpose in life. I have written every page of this book with the sincere prayer that it will have the same effect on you as you read. If you are able to see the simple story that the Bible teaches, it will keep you from wasting your time in trivial arguments and activities and will set you free to invest all your energies into fulfilling your part in God's story.

What you will read in this book is the culmination of over 20 years of hard work as a Bible teacher. It emerged from hours spent with men and women discussing the Bible around kitchen tables and in small group studies where common people were allowed to ask questions. Some of these people had never held a Bible in their hands, many were from other religious backgrounds, while others had attended church for years and read the Bible many times. In spite of their diversity, a common question arose. How can the Bible's message be summed up? Does the Bible have a storyline that threads its way through all the books? Or, is the Bible a random collection of unrelated legends, histories and poems bound up into a single book? This book answers this question.

I wrote the book as a companion to the video teaching. However, it is much more than a transcript. It supplements what you watch in the videos by expanding the teaching and adding lots of Bible references. And, there is additional teaching in the book that is not in the videos. It is written in a simple, conversational style so that the content can be easily understood.

You need to watch the videos, because they are full of fast paced, animated maps, charts, images and Bible texts. There are nine videos and each one is only 12–13 minutes long. Best of all, the videos are available for free on YouTube.[1] While filming, I realized that if I included too many Bible verses the length of the videos would double and the short teaching would become very long. In the end, the simplicity would be lost. Yet, I wanted to include the Bible verses. I believe it is very important for every person to look up the Bible verses, to read each one for themselves and not to blindly accept what I am teaching. When you read the Bible verses for yourself, God will speak to you in ways that I cannot. So, the book is a supplemental companion that beefs up the videos.

What you will learn in this book and video series is what you would be taught at a Bible College. This type of course would be called a "Survey of the Bible" or a "Bible Overview." Don't be fooled by the brief and simple approach used in this book. After reading it, you will not only understand many details of how the story is assembled, but you will see the entire Bible as one book that tells a simple story.

> Then He opened their minds to understand the
> Scriptures (Luke 24:45 NLT).

---

[1] See http://www.youtube.com/c/RichardBustraan for the video series. The Story of the Bible has its own playlist.

Introduction

Jesus Tells the Story

Welcome to this teaching on *The Story of the Bible*. It is a nine-part series. This chapter is the "Introduction." Each one of the next eight chapters will walk you through the parts of the story from Genesis to Revelation. The first five cover the Old Testament, from creation up until four hundred years before Jesus came to earth. The final three cover the New Testament, from the life of Christ into eternity.

Old Testament	New Testament
Prophecies Written	Prophecies Fulfilled

from CREATION ⟶ to 400 BC ✝ — Good News ⟶ ⛥

CHAPTERS 1 – 5　　　**CHAPTERS 6 – 8**

The Story of the Bible in Three Prophecies

Did you know that the Bible tells a story and that this story is summarized in three prophecies? I did not say three themes. Themes are only categories that help us to arrange topics. I said prophecies. Prophecies are God's word telling us in advance what He will do and promising us that He will do it. From Genesis to Revelation there are three prophecies that bring together the simple story that the Bible tells.

The Three Prophecies

1. The first prophecy tells us that someone called the Messiah would come to earth to suffer and die for the sins of all people.

2. The second prophecy tells us that the message of Good News would go to all the people of the earth.

3. The third prophecy tells us that the Messiah will return to earth to be a king forever.

These three prophecies connect all the individual books and stories of the Bible under one umbrella. What I'm saying is this. There are 39 books in the Old Testament. They tell a story of a Messiah who would come into the world to suffer and die. They also tell us that the Good News would go to all nations and that the Messiah would return to earth to be a king. The Old Testament story begins at creation and ends approximately 400 years before Jesus the Messiah came to earth. These three prophecies were given in the Old Testament and they sum up the entire story of the Bible.

There are another 27 books in the Bible called the New Testament. In the New Testament we are introduced to a man named Jesus and told that He was the Messiah spoken about in the Old Testament prophecies. The New Testament also tells about the first sixty years of church history and how the Good News began to spread to all people of the earth. The second prophecy continues to be fulfilled into our day as we see people from every nation being forgiven in the name of Jesus the Messiah. The New Testament also tells us about the future when Jesus the Messiah will return to be a king forever.

We can see that the Bible is actually one book with one story, summarized in three prophecies. The prophecies were made in the Old Testament and they are fulfilled in the New Testament. Jesus is the central character of the Bible and the one who fulfills the prophecies.

If you are unfamiliar with the Bible, you might find it difficult to think of a single verse that demonstrates any of the three prophecies. If you have read the Bible, you may be able to locate a number of verses that would show these three prophecies. In either case, have you ever realized that these three prophecies summarize the entire story of the Bible?

The reason we lose the simplicity of the Bible's story is due to its size. The Bible is a big book. In fact, when you open the Bible you will see sixty–six books, written by more than forty authors over a period of 1500 years. Because we see many authors, many books and many different stories, it is difficult to bring it all together as one, single story. But, I want you to see that the Bible is actually one book that tells one story. It tells us that the Messiah would suffer and die for sins, that the Good News would go to all the nations and that the Messiah would return to set up His kingdom over all the earth.

Q. Do you think that the authors of the Bible were aware that the Bible told a single story?

Do you think that the people who wrote the Bible knew that they were contributing to one main story? Maybe you have never asked yourself this question before, but it is important to understand the answer. The writers of the Bible were aware that the books they wrote were being added to a larger collection and that the stories they told were being joined together to tell a bigger, single story. Each author realized that they were not simply writing an independent book that would make sense on its own. They knew that they were contributing authors, led by God's Spirit to build and develop the story that God was telling. Now, that we have the whole Bible, you and I are able to make sense of the single story.

Jesus Tells the Story of the Bible

A good question to ask is what Jesus would say. After all, He is the main character of the Bible. If He summarized the story of the Bible in three prophecies, it might help to convince you that this is not some theory that I have invented. Does Jesus say anything about the story of the Bible? Yes, He does. In the book of Luke 24:44–47, He tells us the main story.

Before we read these verses, let me explain the context. The words you are about to read were spoken by Jesus after He died on the cross and came back to life. We read in the Bible that before Jesus went into heaven, He spent forty days on earth teaching His disciples about the future and about His coming kingdom. It was during these forty days that Jesus spoke the following words.

> He said to them "This is what I told you while I was still with you. Everything had to be fulfilled that is written about me in the Law of Moses, the Prophets and the Psalms" (Luke 24:44 NIV).

Jesus said that there were prophecies written about Him and that He had fulfilled these prophecies. Where were the prophecies written? Jesus said that they were written in the "Law of Moses, the Prophets and the Psalms." The Law of Moses, the Prophets and the Psalms was the Jewish term for the 39 books of the Old Testament. So, Jesus said that there was prophecy written about Him in the 39 books of the Old Testament. What did Jesus say was written in the Old Testament? Let's keep reading.

Then He opened their minds so they could understand the scripture. He told them, "This is what was written. The Messiah will suffer and rise from the dead on the third day" (Luke 24:45,46).

Did you read what Jesus said? He said that the first of the three prophecies is found in the Old Testament – *"that the Messiah would suffer and rise from the dead on the third day."* And He claimed to be this Messiah who suffered. Next Jesus said,

repentance for the forgiveness of sins will be proclaimed in His name to all people (Luke 24:47).

There is the second prophecy. Jesus said that this second prophecy was part of the Old Testament story – forgiveness of sin would be proclaimed to all people.

But, what about the third prophecy that the Messiah would return to be a king? Did Jesus also teach this? Yes, He did. During this same period of forty days that He was on the earth, Jesus spent a lot of time teaching the apostles about the future and about His coming kingdom (Acts 1:3). It all made sense to the apostles. But they did have one question. When would Jesus return? So they surrounded Jesus and pressed Him for answers about the timing of His return to be a king. The Bible says,

They gathered around him and they asked him, "Lord are you at this time going to restore the kingdom to Israel?" (Acts 1:6 NIV)

Here we read the third prophecy, that Jesus the Messiah will return to be a king and set up His kingdom.

Think about it, during the forty days that Jesus was on earth, before He ascended into heaven, He made sure that the apostles understood how the entire Bible story could be summed up. He opened their eyes so they could understand the Old Testament the way that it was meant to be interpreted. He told them that there were three prophecies that brought together all the other stories and prophecies of the Old Testament. He taught them that He was the Messiah who was to suffer and who would return as a king. In between these two prophecies, they were to take the Good News to all nations. Jesus told them,

> You will receive power when the Holy Spirit comes upon you. And you will be my witnesses, telling people about me everywhere – in Jerusalem, throughout Judea, in Samaria, and to the ends of the earth (Acts 1:8 NLT).

We must remember that when Jesus lived on earth, the only books of the Bible that existed were the 39 books of the Old Testament. The New Testament was being lived out, but it had not been written. This means that Jesus did not introduce a new teaching, but He clarified and summarized the Old Testament the way God had intended it to be. Then, He fulfilled the prophecies made in the Old Testament. Please pay attention to how significant this is. The main character of the Bible, Jesus, summarized the story of the Bible in three prophecies. When the Bible wrote that Jesus *"opened their eyes to understand the scripture,"* it means that Jesus was giving them a way to interpret the entire Old Testament. In fact, He helped them to see the Old Testament the way that the authors had intended. If Jesus the Messiah taught this, then we should embrace His teaching as the best way to sum up the story of the Bible.

A Prayer

> Father, the same way Jesus opened the eyes of the apostles to understand the scripture, open my eyes to see that these three prophecies summarize the story of the Bible. Change my priorities so that my life story becomes part of your story.

The Apostles Tell the Story of the Bible

What about the apostles? What did they teach? If Jesus showed the apostles how to summarize the story of the Bible in three prophecies, then certainly we should expect that they understood and promoted the same message. When we read the apostles teaching, what do we find? We discover that the apostles did tell the story of the Bible the same way that Jesus told it. I want to read two examples from the apostle Peter. One is taken from the beginning and the other from the end of his life. This way you can see that the apostle Peter faithfully taught the three prophecies throughout the course of his entire life.

Let me begin with Acts 3:17–21,24,25. This was the second sermon on record that Peter ever preached. He spoke these words very soon after Jesus had gone into heaven, in the days when the very first believers were assembling in Jerusalem. Notice how Peter included all three prophecies in his teaching. He said,

> Friends, I realize that what you and your leaders did to Jesus was done in ignorance, but God was fulfilling what all the prophets had foretold about the Messiah, that he must suffer these things (Acts 3:17–18 NLT).

Here, Peter mentioned the first prophecy, that the Messiah would suffer, and he claimed that the Old Testament prophets foretold this. Where do you think Peter learned this? Peter continued,

> Now repent of your sins and turn to God so that your sins may be wiped away. Then times of refreshment will come from the presence of the Lord (Acts 3:19).

Notice, this is the second prophecy. The Good News will go to all people. Peter taught his audience that the Good News had reached them and that they needed to turn to God and believe so they could experience the happiness and refreshing that comes from a new heart. Then Peter continued,

> And He [the Father] will again send you Jesus, you're appointed Messiah (Acts 3:20).

Some people find this verse confusing. But, it is very simple. Peter taught that Jesus will come back again. The way Peter said it shows that the Father will send the Son. He will send Jesus the Messiah back to earth. He will return as Messiah the king. Jesus is coming again. In fact, Peter said,

> He must remain in heaven until the time for the final restoration of all things (Acts 3:21).

The "final restoration" refers to the time in the future when the Messiah will return to earth and restore His Kingdom over Israel. So, in Acts 3:20,21, we see that Peter communicated to the people the third prophecy, that Jesus was the Messiah who would return as the king. Before concluding his teaching, he made one last comment.

> Starting with Samuel, every prophet spoke about what is happening today. You are the children of those prophets and you are included in the Covenant God promised our ancestors. For God said to Abraham "through your descendants all families on earth will be blessed" (Acts 3:24,25).

Peter claimed that all the prophets wrote about the events taking place in his day. What were those events? The Messiah had suffered and the Good News began to go to all nations. Peter mentioned Samuel and Abraham who lived 1000 years and 2000 years before his lifetime and he claimed that these two men, and all the other prophets, wrote in advance that the events of Peter's day would take place. He even quoted Genesis 12:3 as the first mention of the promise that the Good News would reach all people. Who taught Peter to summarize the Bible like this? It stands as proof that Peter understood the story of the Bible the way Jesus told it and he taught the same message.

Next, I would like to show you an example that is close to the time of Peter's death to confirm that Peter faithfully taught these three prophecies until the end of his life. Peter wrote,

> This salvation was something even the prophets wanted to know more about when they prophesied about this great salvation prepared for you. They wondered what time or situation the Spirit of Christ within them was talking about when he told them in advance about Christ's suffering and his great glory afterward (1 Peter 1:10,11 NLT).

First, we see that Peter was still teaching the three prophecies: 1) "Christ's suffering," 2) "this great salvation prepared for you,"3) "his great glory afterward."

Second, Peter tells us that the prophets wrote down their visions and revelations and they understood what they wrote. But, they still had questions about the timing and circumstances of their prophecies. They could not figure how to put these three prophecies in sequential order. They asked themselves how the Messiah could suffer and die and at the same time be a king forever? When would the Good News reach all people? What would be happening in the world when the Messiah came to earth? What would be the condition of the human heart? Many years before the events came, the prophets looked into the future and could see them. They partially understood their prophetic writings, but not completely.

We face the same problem when we look into the future. We understand the prophetic writings about the Messiah's suffering and death because these events already happened. We understand the prophecies about the Good News reaching every nation because we see this being fulfilled before our eyes. But the return of the Messiah as a king forever raises many questions. When will He come? In the years leading up to His return, what will be taking place in Israel and in the world? Does He come before, during or after the Great Tribulation? The prophets had this same dilemma, only, they were looking forward in time and trying to make sense of all three prophecies.

So, we see that Peter, one of the apostles, in both his early sermons and in his later writings, understood and taught the same story of the Bible that Jesus taught. Jesus taught all the apostles to see it this way and they taught their followers.

CONCLUSION

The Bible tells a simple story. This story can be summarized under three main prophecies. The first prophecy tells us that someone called the Messiah would come to the earth to suffer and die for the sins of all people. The second prophecy tells us that the message of Good News would go to all the people of all the earth. The Good News is that God will forgive anyone's sin who believes in the Messiah. The third prophecy is that the Messiah will return to earth to be a king forever.

It is true that both the Old and New Testaments teach on countless topics. No one should limit the amazing depth of God's Word to a few simple teachings. However, the Bible does have a main message. When we understand this main message, our understanding of the Bible will be changed forever. It is my goal in this book and video teaching to show you how Jesus and the apostles told the main storyline of the Bible. In the next eight chapters, I will walk you through the whole Bible, showing you where these prophecies were made, how the story developed and the way that these three prophecies formed the narrative for the entire Bible.

FINAL QUESTIONS

Now that we have seen the story of the Bible the way that Jesus and the apostles told it, I want to ask you five questions.

Q. How has this chapter helped you or changed the way that you see the story of the Bible?

Q. Does your church teach and emphasize the story of the Bible the way that Jesus taught it?

Q. Could you imagine sitting at the apostles' feet, listening to them teach from the Old Testament about the Messiah and the Good News? Do you think it would have shaped your perspective any differently than the way you have been taught?

Q. Have you ever thought of yourself as a character in God's story?

Q. Could you find any of the three prophecies in the Old Testament?

CHAPTER ONE

Origins
(Genesis 1–11)

In Chapter One of the Story of the Bible, entitled "Origins," we will overview Genesis chapters 1–11. I want you to see how these eleven chapters are an introduction to the entire Bible setting a backdrop for everything else that is written in the scripture. Remember, we are studying three prophecies and how they summarize the entire story of the Bible.

Creation and Man's Origins

Debates rage over origins. Topics like, where did the heavens and the earth come from? When did they come into existence? Where did human beings come from and when did we come into existence? How did people migrate across the face of the earth? Where did our different cultures and languages come from? Why are there so many differences between races and yet such a common thread that ties all human beings together as one race? Where does evil and death come from? Has human life changed at all since the earliest people walked the face of the earth?

I do not want to avoid these discussions, but the intent of this book and the video series is not to debate origins. Instead, I want to lead us through the narrative presented in the Bible and tell the whole story in its simplicity. So, press the pause button on the questions and arguments over origins for a few moments and enjoy the story that the Bible tells.

Origins / Beginnings

The word Genesis means "origins" or "beginnings." The name comes from the first words of the book that read, "In the beginning" (Genesis 1:1 NIV). Beginnings is the perfect title for the book because in the book of Genesis we read about the origins of things we share in common as human beings. It is true that all over the world we have different cultures, languages, food and music and this is what makes us unique. But, we also share things in common and this is what makes us one human race. We share good things, bad things and a common solution to our main problem and in the book of Genesis we discover where these come from.

The Good

No matter where we come from in the world, we know what it means to see the sunrise and the sunset, to be inspired by the beauty of the mountains, valleys and plains, to eat fruit and vegetables of all kinds and to enjoy all sorts animals. We know what it means to see the moon and the stars and to experience love, marriage and family. Every one of us, no matter where we are from in the world, experiences these good things. Where did all the good things we enjoy come from? The Bible says that God created us and everything. This is what is written.

> In the beginning, God created the heavens and the earth . . .
> Then God said, "Let us make mankind in our image, in our likeness, so that they may rule over the fish in the sea and the birds in the sky, over the livestock and all the wild animals and over all the creatures that move along the ground." So God created mankind in his own image, in the image of God he created them. Male and female he created them. God blessed them and said to them, "Be fruitful and increase in number. Fill the earth and subdue it"

(Genesis 1:1,26–28 NIV).

The most beautiful benefit enjoyed by the first man and woman was their relationship with God. They knew God perfectly. They knew all about Him and experienced His love, His grace, His faithfulness, His gentleness, His beauty and His friendship. In fact, at the end of each day, after God had finished creating everything, He said that it was "good" (Genesis 1:4,10,12,18, 21, 25, 31 NIV). By saying it was good, God meant that all of His creation was perfect. It was complete. It was not lacking anything. There was nothing evil. Everything was exactly the way that God wanted it to be.

The Bad

But, wait a minute! Everything is not good! There are police, courts and jails in all countries, because there is criminal activity in every society. More than this, there is a lot of evil activity in our cultures that you might not go to jail for, but, it is destructive and wicked nonetheless. For example, there is hatred, slander, gossip, lying, cheating, jealousy, lust, greed and adultery. In the end, there is brokenness, betrayal and deep hurt in our relationships. Also, we think many evil thoughts that no one knows about. All is not good. And most important of all, there is one thing that every person experiences, no matter what culture we are from. We all experience death. All of us will meet our appointment with death. So, every person enjoys the good things of life, but also experiences evil, sin and death. If everything was good, where did evil, sin and death come from?

The book of Genesis uncovers the origins of evil, sin and death. It tells us that when God created the first man and woman, He made them perfect and He set them in a garden called Eden. Their names were Adam and Eve. In the Garden of Eden, He provided them with different kinds of trees as their source of food. In fact, they could eat from any tree they wanted, except for one – the tree of the knowledge of good and evil. God said to them, *"You are free to eat from any tree in the garden. But*

you must not eat from the tree of the knowledge of good and evil.
For when you eat from it, you will certainly die." (Genesis 2:17
NIV). But the man and the woman, tempted by Satan, ate the
fruit of that tree anyway and they died. Their relationship with
God was broken. Sin and death entered into the world. They
came under judgment and would forever be separated from God,
unless God himself did something to rescue them.

The book of Genesis tells us that sin, evil and death came
into the world because Adam and Eve disobeyed God and ate
from the tree of the knowledge of good and evil. God gave the
man and the woman a choice to love Him or turn away from Him
and they chose to turn away from Him. This is why God's good
and perfect creation is now tainted and polluted with evil and
why the original, beautiful relationship with God was destroyed.
The result is sad and hopeless. All men and women would never
know God again.

We are the descendants of the first man and woman. But,
we have never known the perfect relationship with God that they
enjoyed. We only know this broken world. We only know a
broken relationship with God. There is a distance between us
and God and we often feel it. Sometimes we wonder if there is a
God. We wonder where God is, if He is listening or if He cares.
We feel abandoned and deserted by God. This is the
consequence of a severed relationship. Worst yet, because of our
sin, after we die, we will face God as our judge, not as our friend.
He will make the final decision about our destiny. This is a
serious problem for all people and without help from God, we
will live forever in suffering and torment. What can we do?

There is ample evidence of this in every culture. For
example, I have lived on four continents and I have seen with
my own eyes the behavior of children. Children naturally do
wrong. All over the world, parents correct wrong behavior and
try to teach their children to do what is right. This is because
children, from their nature, tell lies, are greedy for other
children's toys and know how to punch, kick and bite others.
Don't misunderstand me. Kids are lovely and I do not say this to

belittle children. I only say this to prove a point. All people, in every culture, inherit a sinful nature from Adam and Eve. It is in our genes when we are born. We openly sin when we are young and, as we age, we become remarkably sophisticated at doing evil and hiding it. We are sinners by birth. In addition, I have attended funerals in many cultures and seen that death happens in all cultures. And I have talked to people from many cultures who express a deep, inner pain from being lonely, people who admit they cannot feel God's presence. All this is evidence that we as human beings share a common problem of sin, death and a severed relationship with God. The Bible tells us sin came from Adam and Eve.

The Solution

Although the problem is great, God has created a solution that will bring us back to Himself and save us from this terrible, eternal destiny. He promised that He would send a Savior, a Messiah, someone to rescue us from this tragic end. The story of the Bible moves along very quickly and already, by Genesis chapter three, God has introduced His solution to our human problem. God presented it in a conversation between Himself and Satan immediately after the man and the woman made the terrible decision to eat the fruit of the tree of the knowledge of good and evil. Sin and death had entered into Adam and Eve. But, instead of speaking words of gloom and judgment, God spoke words of hope and salvation. He said.

> I will put enmity between you and the woman, between your offspring and hers. He will crush your head and you will strike His heel (Genesis 3:15 NIV).

This brief, powerful prophecy was spoken to Satan about his ultimate downfall and about the coming of the Messiah. From this verse, we learn three important truths. First, the Messiah will be a human being who comes from Eve. Notice that God said there will be an antagonistic and hostile relationship between Satan's people and Eve's offspring. The word "offspring" does not mean all humanity. Although Eve was the first woman and is the mother of every human being, the word "offspring" is pointing to an individual human being who would come to earth in the future. This human being is the Messiah.

Second, we learn that the Messiah will be a male. God said to Satan, *"He will crush your head."* Third, we learn that the Messiah will suffer in order to defeat Satan. God said, *"He will crush your head. You will strike his heel."* Summing up the prophecy of Genesis 3:15, it states that the Messiah will destroy Satan and that Satan will cause the Messiah to suffer. This is very helpful. From the beginning of the Bible a prophetic event has been forecast. If Genesis 3:15 was the only Bible verse we had in our possession, we could conclude that the storyline of the Bible is going to develop around a single, future event that would solve man's greatest needs. The Messiah will suffer to forgive sin and defeat Satan.

To summarize, we see the origins of the good things in life. God created them all. Second, we discover the origins of the bad things in life. Evil, sin, death, the problems in our societies and the distance that we feel from God are all a result of Adam and Eve's choice to disobey God. Finally, we see the origins of God's solution to send a man who will provide a way for all people to be rescued. Pay very close attention to this person who will come from Eve. We are going to follow the storyline of the Bible from this point in Genesis and trace the family tree of this person who will come and rescue us.

Q. Why do you think there are so many genealogies (family trees) in the Bible?

Genealogies / Family Trees

If I handed you a pencil and paper and asked you to write a brief summary of the origins of the earth and human life, would you ever think to include genealogies? Yet, when you read the Bible, you will discover chapters devoted to family trees. Have you ever asked yourself why? In fact, in the first eleven chapters of Genesis, we are told a story about the origins of the earth, a flood that destroyed all human life and how the people of the earth migrated to their present locations. These are hugely significant events in the origins of life on the planet. But, Genesis chapters five, ten and much of eleven are family trees. Why is there so much emphasis on genealogies? The answer is simple. The Bible is tracing the family line of the Messiah, beginning with Eve, the first woman. From Genesis 3:15, the Bible's story begins to take shape around this promise and this family line. The genealogies in the Bible begin with Eve and end with Jesus the Messiah. By tracing the family line from Eve to Jesus, Bible genealogies demonstrate that Jesus was the Messiah who came to crush the head of Satan. After Jesus the Messiah came to earth 2000 years ago, there were no more genealogies.

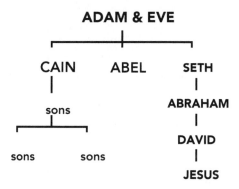

The genealogies trace the family line of Eve to Jesus the Messiah.

The World Before the Flood

By Genesis 4, we already read about a murder spurred on by jealousy. In chapter five the earth, which was probably one supercontinent or Pangea, began to fill with all kinds of people. By counting the generations in the genealogical record, many scholars have determined there to be 1600 years of human life before the flood. While no one claims to know the world population at that time, I have read guesses that range from 200 million to several billion people.[2] In either case, by reading the narrative with a creative imagination we have a better chance at painting an accurate picture of the world's population and human achievement during this era of human history. In other words, the Bible does not suggest that there were only a few thousand grunting, prehistoric cave people populating a remote forest region of the planet. In fact, Genesis chapters five and six give the impression that the earth was full of people, bustling with activity and very progressive.

However, in chapter six we read that the earth had become very evil and the Bible especially highlights a formidable level of violence (Genesis 6:11–13). As a result, we read one of the saddest comments on humanity that exists in the entire Bible. Listen to what God said about the world in those days.

> The Lord saw how great the wickedness of the human race had become on earth and that every inclination of the thoughts of the human heart was only evil, all the time (Genesis 6:6 NIV).

As a result, God responded with a timeline of judgment. The Bible writes,

---

[2] By counting the years mentioned in the genealogies, many say there were exactly 1656 years between creation and the flood. I am not interested in presenting arguments for or against a particular view on pre–flood world populations. It makes for entertaining discussion, but determining the population of the earth before the flood has little bearing on the narrative.

The Lord regretted that he had made human beings on the earth, and his heart was deeply troubled. So the Lord said, "I will wipe from the face of the earth the human race I have created – and with them the animals, the birds and the creatures that move along the ground – for I regret that I have made them." But Noah found favor in the eyes of the Lord (Genesis 6:6–8 NIV).

The Flood

Quite a sad outcome. The increasing levels of evil in the human race provoked God to respond in judgment. What we read next is an account of a worldwide flood and how God judged the world by covering it with water and destroying every living thing. It takes four chapters, Genesis six through nine, to give the details of the flood account. This means that the Bible tells us more about the flood than it does about creation. While many people debate the origins of the earth and humanity, the Bible highlights this sudden, catastrophic event in the history of the world, called the flood, with equal significance. It writes about what took place, who was rescued and the reasons why it happened.

Did you know that people groups all over the world tell stories about the origins of the earth and of man? What is equally fascinating is that most cultures around the world have accounts of the flood and how God rescued one man and his family from the judgment of water. Not a few of these accounts also tell a story of people migrating across the face of the earth, after the global flood. These stories serve to reinforce cultural identities by explaining how they arrived on their tribal lands and why they occupy them. These uncollaborated stories are evidence in our human cultures that a worldwide flood did occur. In fact, many within the communities of archaeology, geology and paleontology agree that there was a recent and catastrophic event that altered the structure and ecological system of the entire world. The Bible shows us this event was called the flood.

Three Truths from the Flood

There are three main lessons we learn from the flood. First, we learn about God's judgment. God is amazingly patient, but His patience does not last forever. God sets a time for judgment. He stops all human activity and brings every person to account for their life. In the days leading up to the flood, the population of the world increased and so did the level of violence and evil (Genesis 6:1,5,11–13). God's patience wore thin and He decided He would no longer wrestle against the evil and violence of humanity (Genesis 6:3). He established a timeline of 120 years (Genesis 6:3) and began to count down the years until the day that He would flood the earth with water and kill every living thing. During this 120 years, Noah prepared the ark and warned the people that God's countdown to judgment had begun. In fact, the Bible calls Noah a preacher of righteousness (2 Peter 2:5).

The flood is not the only judgment mentioned in Scripture. Another time of judgment is predicted for the near future, when God will judge the earth and all humanity with fire. So, the flood stands as a warning for us who live today. The same way that God warned the world in Noah's day that in 120 years, He would send a flood, God warns us that He will judge the world with fire at some point in the near future (2 Peter 3:1–16).

Second, we learn about God's salvation. Although God killed every living thing in the flood, He preserved eight people – Noah, his wife, Noah's three sons and their wives. The ark, the large boat that Noah built, rescued them from being drown along with the rest of humanity. By saving them, He saved the human race and He saved the family line of the Messiah, the person He promised would bring salvation to the earth. God wants to save. The Lord says,

I take no pleasure in the death of the wicked, but
rather that they turn from their ways and live
(Ezekiel 33:11 NLT).

Third, we learn about faith. Put yourself in Noah's sandals for a
moment. God asked Noah to build a boat, a really big boat.
Instead of building the boat near a lake or near the sea, he built
this huge boat in the middle of a field. Then God told Noah it
was going to rain. From the day God created the earth until the
days of Noah, it had never rained. What amazing faith Noah had,
to trust God to do what He said He would do. He trusted that
God would send rain and flood the earth when Noah had never
seen rain. Because he believed that God would send rain, Noah
built the boat. In fact, the ark was one of the largest boats ever
built until the 1800s. Because Noah believed, he was saved.
Jesus the Messiah is like the ark. If we believe in Him, we will
be rescued through Him from the judgment of fire.

 What does the flood teach us about judgment,
salvation and faith?

People Migrate Across the Earth

After the flood, God promised all people that He would never
again destroy the world with water. When the flood waters
subsided, the surface of the earth had been transformed and in
the place of one supercontinent, there were many continents.
This was God's way of breaking up the earth into different
locations for people to inhabit. Soon after the flood, as people
began to increase in number, they still shared one common
language and culture and they were determined to remain one
people. However, God confused their language and, by default,
humanity was divided up into many linguistic and cultural
groupings and began to migrate across the face of the earth. This

shows us something really wonderful about God. Although we belong to one human race, God approves of our diverse cultures and languages. It pleases Him to see the world filled with one human race that has different cultures, speaking different languages and having many unique identities. The following Bible verse makes this very clear.

> From one man, He made all the nations, that they should inhabit the whole earth. He marked out their appointed times in history and the boundaries of their lands. God did this so that they would seek him and perhaps reach out for him and find him, though he is not far from any one of us (Acts 17:26–27 NIV).[3]

Isn't this verse beautiful? God has made many people groups from Adam and Eve. He has appointed a time for each people to rise with power and then to decline. He has also apportioned land to each different people as property boundaries where they can live. For every people group around the world, the land where they live is one way that they define who they are.

Notice that the Bible also states that God is not far from any one of us. God wants us to seek Him and reach out to Him. But more than reaching and seeking, He also wants us to find Him. When we find God, we find life. When we find God, we find a new heart. When we find God, we will find the solution to our sin problem.

CONCLUSION

Genesis 1–11 raises some really big questions about the origins of the earth, the origins of man, the age of the earth, the age of humanity, the flood and people migration. These are very

---

[3] The word "nations" means ethnic people groups.

important issues. But, these topics are much more than can be handled in this brief chapter and in the 12–minute video. The intention of this book and video is to introduce you to the story of the Bible and the purpose of this chapter is to show you how Genesis chapters 1–11 set the backdrop for the rest of scripture.

I would like to wrap up Chapter 1, "Origins," Genesis 1–11. We are examining the story of the Bible as Jesus and the apostles told it. According to them, the entire Bible can be summarized in three prophecies. First, someone called the Messiah would come to earth and He would suffer and die for sin. Second, the Good News would go to all nations. Third, the Messiah will return as a king. In this chapter, we see the story begin with all the good things that God made. We learn where evil and sin came from and how lost we are as human beings. We learn about the promise made to Eve that a descendant will come from her, a male child, who will bring salvation. We read the most detailed historical account ever produced about the flood and we see how much God affirms our diverse cultures. The stage is now set for the Messiah's blessing to reach all people on earth, no matter where we are from.

FINAL QUESTIONS

Q. How did we develop so many different cultures, if all people came from one man and woman?

Q. Do you think it really matters if we as human beings were created by God or evolved from lifeless matter?

Q. Do you think the earth has become as violent as it was in Noah's day, just before God sent the flood?

When the Son of Man returns, it will be like it was in Noah's day. In those days before the flood, the people were enjoying banquets and parties and weddings right up to the time Noah entered his boat. People didn't realize what was going to happen until the flood came and swept them all away. That is the way it will be when the Son of Man comes (Matthew 24:37–39 NLT).

CHAPTER TWO

A Chosen Man – Abraham

(Genesis 12–50)

Abraham

While people were migrating across the face of the earth and inhabiting the lands that were prepared for them, God had his eye on one man. This man lived in a small town called Ur, which is near present day Nasiriyah in Iraq. His name was Abraham. Four thousand years ago, God reached into our world and selected this man Abraham and made promises to him. It is essential that you understand these promises, because the Bible, from this point on, is a story of God fulfilling the promises He made to Abraham. The Bible never does give a reason why God chose Abraham and from what we understand, Abraham seemed to be minding his own business in Ur when the Lord first spoke to him. The Bible tells us that this was God's plan to choose him and that is why he is called "a chosen man."

Abraham Leaves His Home

The Lord appeared to Abraham and asked him to leave his people and to go to a new land that would be given to him. The land was called Canaan, but, it would eventually be renamed Israel, after Abraham's grandson. Knowing nothing about this land, Abraham listened to the Lord and left his family, his culture and everything that was familiar to him. He set out on a long journey up the Euphrates River, across what is Northern Iraq and Syria and ended up in Israel. The long voyage of approximately 1000 miles (1600 kilometers) was not made in an air conditioned car, but on foot, donkeys and camels. And upon his arrival, there was no welcoming party to greet him. To make matters worse, Abraham was not a young man. The Bible tells us that he was just shy of 75 years old when he left Ur. And, as far as we know, he had never before ventured outside the region of Ur. This was an unimaginably enormous act of faith. He left home. He trusted God to do what He said He would do. This is what the Bible says.

> It was by faith that Abraham obeyed when God called him to leave home and go to another land that God would give him as his inheritance. He went without knowing where he was going (Hebrews 11:8 NLT).

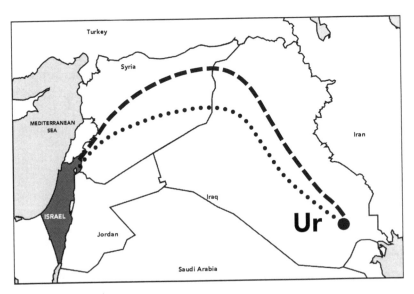

Dotted and dashed lines are proposed routes for Abraham's journey from Ur to Israel (1000 miles/1600 kilometers).

Promises to Abraham

The God of the Bible is a promise maker and a promise keeper. Think about it, God made these promises 4000 years ago and He has not forgotten them. In fact, He is still fulfilling these promises today. Because God is a promise maker and promise keeper, it makes Him different than any other god on earth. All other gods ask their followers to prove their devotion to Him by their actions, by their commitment or by making and fulfilling vows. But, the God of the Bible does not ask you what you can do for Him. He tells you what He will do for you. He asks you if you will trust Him to do what He said He will do. He promises to do something wonderful for you and through you.

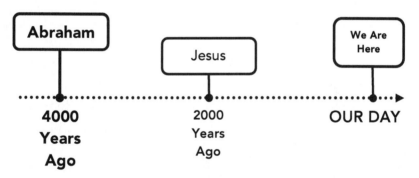

Timeline showing when Abraham lived

What were the promises that God made to Abraham? First, God promised Abraham land. As mentioned earlier, Abraham left his homeland and His own people to go to the land that God showed him. This land is called Israel. Second, God promised Abraham that his family would grow into a nation. This nation is also called Israel. Third, God promised that He would make

Abraham famous. Fourth, God promised Abraham that the Messiah would come through his family line. Fifth, God promised that He would bless Abraham. As you read through the book of Genesis, you will see how incredibly blessed Abraham was. For example, Abraham's "household," which included all his servants and helpers, was probably more than 1000 in number. He possessed scores of herds of livestock and abounded in financial wealth. Finally, the blessing on Abraham was not limited to him, because God promised Abraham that all people on the earth would be blessed through him.

An Example of the Promises

God repeated the promises to Abraham eight different times. I have selected an example from these eight times and I have broken it down to show you the various parts. The example is from Genesis 12:1–3. This was the first time God made the promise to Abraham.

The promise to give Abraham the land.
The Lord said to Abraham, "Leave your native country, your relatives and your father's family and go to the land I will show you" (Genesis 12:1 NLT).

The promise to make Abraham into a nation.
I will make you into a great nation (Genesis 12:2).

The promise to bless Him.
And I will bless you (Genesis 12:2).

The promise to make Abraham famous.
I will make you famous (Genesis 12:2).

> *He lived four thousand years ago and you and I are studying his life. That definitely makes him famous.*

The promise to protect Abraham
You will be a blessing to others and I will bless those
who bless you and I will curse those who curse you
(Genesis 12:2,3).

The promise of Good News to all people
All families on earth will be blessed through you
(Genesis 12:3).

Abraham's Family Line

Abraham had a son named Isaac and a grandson named Jacob.
These three men are called the patriarchs. Anytime you read
about the "patriarchs" or about the "fathers," it is referring to
these three men. God Himself spoke the promises to Abraham,
then to Isaac and then to Jacob. By doing so, God made it clear
that it was not Abraham's idea to pass along the promise to Isaac
and for Isaac to pass along the promise to Jacob. This would be
nothing more than these men blessing each other and attempting
to establish themselves as influential people. Instead, since God
spoke the promises to each of the patriarchs, we understand that
the Lord was the one who established Abraham's family line as
the family of the Messiah.

The promises are so foundational to the rest of the story of
the Bible that the Lord spoke them ten times to these men. The
first eight times He spoke them to Abraham and the last two
times He made the promises to Isaac and to Jacob. Let's briefly
see each of the ten times to understand a little bit about the
context.

The Promises Spoken 10 Times to the Patriarchs

1. Genesis 12:1–3 – God spoke to Abraham when he was in Ur.

2. Genesis 13:14–18 – Lot separated from Abraham because
there were not sufficient pasturelands to feed both men's

livestock. Given the choice, Lot took the best land, the fertile Jordan plain. However, the Lord spoke to Abraham saying that it did not matter which land Lot had chosen. It would never belong to Lot. God promised Abraham all the land that Lot had chosen and much more. The promises were spoken in their complete form.

3. Genesis 15:17–21 – Abraham complained because God had promised to make a nation out of his descendants. But so far, Abraham did not even have one son and he was getting old. God reassured Abraham that his family descendants would be more numerous than the stars in the heaven. Then God made a vow to Abraham that He would keep the promise He made. The vow involved a smoking fire pot and a burning torch. God repeated the promise to him.

4. Genesis 17:1–8; 19–22 – In this chapter God repeated the promise to Abraham and guaranteed that the land of Israel would belong to his descendants forever. Then He commanded Abraham to circumcise all the males in his household. Circumcision was a sign that God promised Abraham the land, the nation, fame, blessing, descendants and that the Good News would go to all people of the earth. Every time a Jewish male saw that he had been circumcised, he was reminded of the promises that God had made to Abraham and that the land was theirs forever.

5. Genesis 18:16–19 – In this story, God revealed to Abraham that it would only be one more year before his son would be born. He also revealed that He would destroy Sodom and Gomorrah where Lot lived. The Lord revealed His plan to destroy the two cities because of the promises He had made to Abraham.

6. Genesis 21:12 – Abraham sent his son Ishmael and his servant Hagar away from his house. Abraham was broken–hearted and God comforted Him with the words that "Isaac is the son through whom your descendants will be counted."

7. Genesis 22:15–18 – Abraham offered his son Isaac as a sacrifice to God. But God provided a lamb as a substitute to die instead of Isaac. After the lamb was offered as a sacrifice, the Lord repeated the entire promise to Abraham.

8. Genesis 24:6,7 – Abraham remembered the promises and used these promises as an assurance that God would provide a wife for his son Isaac from his own people back in Ur.

9. Genesis 26:1–6 – Isaac moved to Gerar, a chief city among the Philistine people. God warned Isaac not to go further south into Egypt. Why? The land had been promised to Abraham and He wanted Isaac to remain in the region. This was the time when God Himself spoke the promises to Isaac that were given to Abraham.

10. Genesis 28:1–17 (especially 13–15) – After Jacob had deceitfully betrayed his brother Esau, he fled from his family because he feared Esau's revenge. Before leaving his family, his father Isaac blessed Jacob with God's blessing. But he also told Jacob, *"May he give you and your descendants the blessing given to Abraham, so that you may take possession of the land where you now reside as a foreigner, the land God gave to Abraham"* (Genesis 28:4 NIV). On his way to Ur, Jacob passed through Haran and in Genesis 28:13–15, the famous "stairway to heaven" passage, God spoke the entire promise to Jacob. The stairway to heaven was the moment when the Lord himself passed the promises along to Jacob.

The Promises Fulfilled in the Bible

The writers of the Bible were aware that the whole story rested on God's ability to fulfill the promises to Abraham, Isaac and Jacob. As a result, the promises to the patriarchs are mentioned so many times that it is impossible to catalogue all the references here. But, I want to show three examples of how other Bible writers point back to the promises to remind us that God is at work fulfilling the promises He made. The first example is from the days of Moses. Four hundred years after the promises were spoken, this small family had become a large nation called Israel. Israel found themselves in Egypt, crushed under oppressive slavery. When God decided it was time to deliver them and bring them into the land that He had promised their forefathers, He raised up Moses to lead His people back into the land of Israel. Notice that the patriarchs are mentioned in the following words.

> But the Israelites continued to groan under their burden of slavery. They cried out for help, and their cry rose up to God. God heard their groaning and He remembered His covenant promise to Abraham, Isaac and Jacob (Exodus 2:23,24 NLT).

The second example occurs 1000 years after the promises were made to the patriarchs. Notice how the writer was aware of the promises and understood that God remembered and was fulfilling the promises.

> Oh offspring of Abraham, his servant, children of Jacob, his chosen ones! He is the Lord our God. His judgments are in all the earth. He remembers his covenant forever, the word that he commanded, for a thousand generations, the covenant that he made with Abraham, his sworn promise to Isaac, which he confirmed to Jacob as a statute, to Israel as an everlasting covenant, saying, "To you I will give the land of Canaan as your portion for an inheritance" (Psalms 105:6–11 ESV).

Third, 2000 years after the promises were made to the patriarchs, the Apostle Paul quoted from Genesis 12:3 and confirmed that

God was fulfilling the promise to Abraham by bringing the Good News to all people of the earth.

> The Scriptures looked forward to this time when God would make the Gentiles [the non–Jewish people] right in His sight because of their faith. God proclaimed this Good News to Abraham long ago when He said, "All nations will be blessed through you" (Galatians 3:8 NLT).

I have only listed three examples, yet they demonstrate a profound point. As centuries passed, the Bible did not become a collection of random stories and unconnected events. Instead, the different authors of the many books believed that there was a single story of a faithful, promise making God, who was fulfilling His promises to the patriarchs. The next time you read through the Bible notice how many times the writers refer back to the promises that God made to the patriarchs.

The Promise of Faith

There is another promise that God made to Abraham called the promise of faith. The promise of faith means that God sees you and me as perfect people, because we believe that He can do what He promised He would do. To say it another way, we are forgiven and accepted by God for one reason, our faith. God has provided a sacrifice for our sins, but He expects us to respond. The response He requires is that we believe. This is a personal decision that each one makes. No one can force you. You are not born into this condition. It does not depend on the religion of your parents or grandparents. To be forgiven, every person must make a personal decision to receive the gift that God is offering.

In the Old Testament and in the New Testament, God forgives, accepts and sees any person as perfect because they believe. This is true all throughout the Bible. Those who lived before Jesus the Messiah looked forward in time and believed that God was going to send a Messiah to die for them. Those of us who live after the death and resurrection of Jesus the Messiah, look back in time and believe that His death pays for our sin. They looked forward in time and we look back in time, but all of us are looking to the Messiah's death as God's provision of a sacrifice for sin. The promise of faith teaches us that all people of all time are accepted by God because they believe that He will do what He promised.

Let me show you an example of faith from Abraham's life. It is found in Genesis 15. At this point in his life, Abraham did not have a child. If he didn't have a child, how could God bring a nation through him? How could God bring the Messiah through his family line? Abraham was already old and so he began to complain to God about his childless condition. Look what the Lord did next.

> Then the Lord took Abram outside and said to him,
> "Look up into the sky and count the stars if you can.
> That's how many descendants you will have"
> (Genesis 15:5 NLT).

Before Abraham had a son, God promised him that his descendants would be as numerous as the stars. Abraham responded to the Lord with simple faith. He heard what the Lord said and he believed that God had the power to do what He said He would do.

> Abram believed the Lord and the Lord counted him
> as righteous because of his faith (Genesis 15:6
> NLT).

The result was simple. The Lord considered Abraham to be a perfect person. It was by faith that Abraham was accepted by God and not because of his good works. Did you know that Abraham died without seeing these promises fulfilled? Don't get me wrong, he did receive a son named Isaac. But, he did not see the nation of Israel. He did not see the Messiah. He did not see you and me being blessed with salvation. He went to his grave believing that God was going to accomplish His plan in the future. That is faith. Not seeing the promise completed, He still trusted that God would fulfill His word. This is the promise of faith. *"Everyone who believes in him will have eternal life"* (John 3:15). You believe and you receive eternal life. You believe and God sees you as perfect. The wonderful promise of faith is first seen in Abraham's life and it continues up to our day.

To summarize, the promise of faith means that God's real children are the people who believe in the Messiah for salvation. We might be tempted to think of the Jewish people as the only children of Abraham, but the Bible teaches that it is the believers in Jesus the Messiah who are the children of Abraham. This is what is written.

> The real children of Abraham, then, are those who put their faith in God (Galatians 3:7 NLT).

> So the promise is received by faith. It is given as a free gift. And we are all certain to receive it, whether or not we live according to the law of Moses, if we have faith like Abraham's. For Abraham is the father of all who believe (Romans 4:16 NLT).

CONCLUSION

Let's conclude chapter 2 by focusing on the family line of Judah and a prophecy that the Messiah would come through his descendants. We must not forget that we are tracing the genealogy of the Messiah and in the closing chapters of Genesis we find another reminder. Abraham had a son named Isaac. Isaac had a son named Jacob and Jacob had 12 sons. One of Jacob's 12 sons was named Judah and it is through Judah that the Messiah would come. This is what the Bible states.

> The scepter will not depart from Judah nor the
> ruler's staff from his descendants, until the coming
> of the one to whom it belongs. The one whom all the
> nations will honor . . . He washes his clothes in wine,
> his robes in the blood of grapes (Genesis 49:10,11).

These prophetic words were spoken by Jacob over his son Judah.
In this prophecy we see that someone in Judah's family line will
hold the "scepter" and the "ruler's staff." The scepter and ruler's
staff are the large rod that a family member would hold in his
hand as a symbol of power, authority and leadership. In addition,
Jacob said that "all the nations will honor" this person.
Amazingly, we also read that this person who comes from
Judah's family line will wash his robes in blood. This means that
the Messiah will shed his blood and die. How incredible. Two
thousand years before Jesus the Messiah came to earth, Jacob
prophesied that the Messiah would be one of Judah's
descendants and that he would both die and be a king over all
the nations.

Through the book of Genesis, we have been tracing the
family line of the Messiah that began with Eve, continued
through Abraham and has been narrowed down to Judah. We
read that the Messiah would die and be a king over all nations.
We learned the promises God made to the patriarchs and how
central these promises are to the story of the Bible. We also
learned about the response that God requires from any person
who wants to be accepted by Him. It is the response of faith.

Examples of the Three Prophecies from Genesis

1. The Messiah would come to earth to suffer and die for sin.

Spoken to Eve

He will crush your head, and you will strike his heel
(Genesis 3:15 NIV).

2. The Good News will go to all nations.

Spoken to Abraham

All people on earth will be blessed through you (Genesis 12:3 NLT).

3. The Messiah will come to earth as a king.

Spoken to Judah

The scepter will not depart from Judah, nor the ruler's staff from between his feet, until he to whom it belongs shall come and the obedience of the nations shall be his. He ties his foal to a grapevine, the colt of his donkey to a choice vine. He washes his clothes in wine, his clothes in the blood of grapes (Genesis 49:10,11 NLT).

FINAL QUESTIONS

Q. What are you trusting God to do for you?

Q. Do you want God to accept you as one of His? How can you be accepted by God?

Q. What has God promised He would do for you?

Q. Can you name some of the promises that God made to Abraham?

CHAPTER THREE

A Chosen Nation – Israel
(Exodus – Judges)

It has taken two chapters to review one book of the Bible, so you might think the story is moving at a snail's pace. But don't worry, this slow moving coach is about to become an express train as we race through the remaining 65 books of the Bible. As the study moves on, keep in mind that the book of Genesis has laid the foundation for the rest of the Bible. This cannot be understated. Genesis has answered many questions about why the Messiah must come to the world. It explains our origins, the causes of evil and death and how God is working a plan to rescue us from judgment. A skeletal framework for the three prophecies has been constructed and now we will begin to put more meat on the bones.

Reading through the books of Exodus to Judges, you'll notice that the spotlight is on the nation of Israel, the chosen nation, and the storyline of these books centers around the law and the land. There is a 300–year gap between the books of Genesis and Exodus and the Bible is silent about what took place during this time.[4] Genesis ends with the account of a family story, 75 members in all, with one of Jacob's 12 sons, Judah, being singled out as the person through whom the Messiah

---

[4] In Genesis 15:13, the Lord told Abraham his descendants would be in Egypt for 400 years. In Exodus 12:40,41, Moses counted Israel's time in Egypt as 430 years, to the very day. In Galatians 3:17, the apostle Paul said that there were 430 years between the promises to Abraham and the Old Covenant at Mount Saini in Exodus 24. The 300–year gap is not approximated on the time in Egypt, but on the silence between the books of Genesis and Exodus.

would come. Jacob, his sons and grandsons made their way down to Egypt to survive a famine and settle in the lush, fertile region of Goshen.

When you open the book of Exodus, it is no longer a family story, but a national story. The family of 75 grew to be a people that numbered around 2 million. At this time in their history, they were a tribal people with no king as their leader. Immediately, Moses is introduced as the man that God chose to lead the people of Israel out of Egypt and into the land that He had promised to give to Abraham, Isaac and Jacob. The exit from their 400 year stay in Egypt came at great cost to the Egyptian people. Devastating plagues were unleashed by God in an attempt to persuade a fickle and hard–hearted Egyptian leader, called Pharaoh, to give the Jewish people permission to leave. Finally, Pharaoh released Israel and Moses led them out of the region of Goshen and to a mountain in the wilderness called Sinai. Scholars believe Sinai is located in one of two places, one at the tip of the Sinai Peninsula and the other in Southern Saudi Arabia.[5]

Three months after leaving Egypt, the people of Israel found themselves at the base of Mount Sinai and there they entered into an agreement with God that is called "The Old Testament" or "The Old Covenant."[6] The agreement was instituted in Exodus chapter 24. The ceremony at Sinai etched in stone an arrangement between God and the Jewish people that determined the outcome of their history and explains the reason why God sent prophets years later. We will return to Exodus 24 and unpack the meaning of the Old Covenant in just a moment. But first, I want to finish the remainder of the story of the books of Exodus to Judges.

What happened next was very disappointing. The nation of Israel was supposed to move from Mount Sinai and enter

---

[5] From 1 Kings 6:1, we can determine the date of the Exodus as 3446 years ago. Construction on the Temple began 2967 years ago. Add to this, 479 years to get 3446 years ago.
[6] Both phrases mean the same thing.

directly into the land that God had promised to the patriarchs. As they neared the borders of the promised land, scouts were sent in advance to explore and report back encouraging words of hope and blessing that lay ahead. But, instead of encouraging the people to have faith and move into the land, the reports soured the hearts of the people and they decided that God did not have the power to give them the land. God told them that if they did not believe that He had the power to give them the land, then they would remain in the desert and die there. And that is exactly what happened. The next generation was the generation that entered and conquered the land. But they had to wait 40 years for every member of the faithless generation to pass away. The books of Exodus, Leviticus, Numbers and Deuteronomy give the account of Israel's 40 years in the wilderness.

In the book of Joshua, we read about a man named Joshua. He succeeded Moses and led the next generation of people into the land. After exiting the desert and crossing the Jordan River, he led Israel into three main battle operations. The first campaign conquered the southern region of Israel. The second took the central region and the third overthrew the people in the northern areas of Israel. The book of Joshua is primarily about the promised land being conquered, divided up and apportioned to the 12 tribes.

Next is the book of Judges. It spans 350 years.[7] When reading Judges, you will observe a pattern. Israel would turn away from the Lord and live an evil lifestyle. As a result, they would be enslaved by the nations that lived as their neighbors. After a season of cruel oppression, the people would cry out to God, who in turn would raise up a judge to deliver the people. Throughout the book of Judges, the people were ruled regionally by tribal leaders and the judge acted as a national leader. But, no dynasty was established to maintain a family line for the judges.

---

[7] Determining the number of years of Judges varies depending on a number of factors, like the overlap in dates of the books of Ruth and 1 Samuel and whether or not Samuel is considered to be a Judge. See academic note at the end of the book for an explanation of dates.

When the judge passed away, it was the end of his rule. Israel was rescued from their tyranny, but in time would turn away from God again. This pattern is repeated numerous times.

However, there was something else taking place in the story of Judges that is seldom realized. Every time God raised up a judge to deliver the people of Israel, more land would be conquered and the boundaries of Israel continued to expand. Little by little, God was fulfilling His promise to Abraham, Isaac and Jacob to give their descendants the land of Canaan and to make them into a nation. The stage was being set for the Messiah to come to earth and for the blessing to be brought to every people group in the world. The books of Exodus to Judges cover a 500–year period of time, from 3500 years ago until 3000 years ago (approximately).[8]

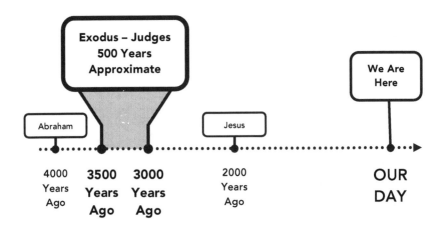

Timeline showing the period of Exodus to Judges

---

[8] Adding 80 years, Moses' age at the Exodus, to the date of the Exodus, 3446 years ago, gives a date of 3526 years ago.

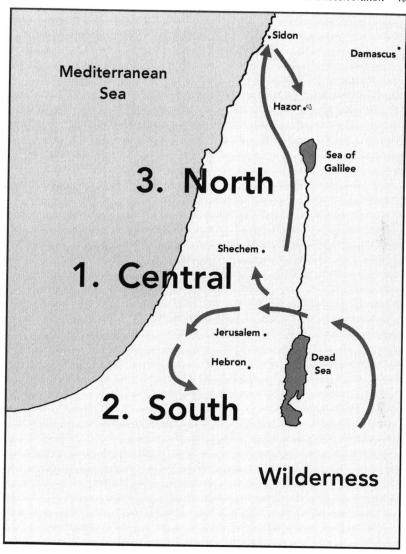

Joshua led Israel into Promised Land

Joshua led Israel from the wilderness (bottom right) into the promised land. His first series of battles conquered the central region, indicated (1). The second conquered the southern region, indicated (2). The third reached as far north as Sidon and Hazor, indicated (3).

Names of Judges and their location

During the days of the Judges, Israel continued to conquer more of the land promised to Abraham, Isaac and Jacob. The book of Judges covers approximately 300 years. Some include Samuel as a Judge, which would make the time of the Judges slightly longer.

The Law

With this brief history in place, let's return to Old Covenant and consider exactly what it meant. Let me start by giving you three helpful tips. First, as I discuss the Law, sometimes I will call it the Law and sometimes the Law of Moses. Second, if you understand the Law, you will be able to make sense of what is called the "Old Covenant" or "The Old Testament." For many people, even after attending church for years, there is a lot of confusion about the Old Covenant. When asked what the Old Covenant is, when it took place or where it is located in the Bible, few can answer with confidence. So, I want to clarify this for you. Third, you will be able to understand the purpose behind the prophets and why the story of the Old Testament works out the way it does. So, give this your best attention and I will make every effort to keep it simple.

When we think of the Law, we usually think of the 10 commandments. But, did you know there are 613 commandments in the Law of Moses? And, it was much more than an incredibly long list of regulations to simply make people follow rules. It guided all of Israel's daily life and bound Israel in a lease agreement. In the following paragraphs, I want to show you how to break down the Law of Moses into three parts 1) the Ceremonial, 2) the Civil and 3) the Moral Law. And I want to show you how the Law served as a lease agreement between the Lord and Israel over the promised land.

The Ceremonial Law

The Ceremonial Law guided the religious life of Israel and centered around the Tabernacle. The Tabernacle was a portable tent where God was worshiped. We learn how Israel was to build the Tabernacle, how they should carry it and how they should furnish it.[9] It gave instructions to the priests about how they should live, about their clothing and what their work involved.[10] It also gave instructions on dietary regulations outlining what the Jewish people could and could not eat.[11] There were instructions on religious festivals, both how and when these should be carried out.[12] It gave guidance on sacrifices and worship around the temple, the types of offerings to be offered, the way the offerings were to be performed and who was to perform them.[13]

The Bible tells us that Jesus the Messiah has fulfilled the Ceremonial Law and so we do not have to obey these regulations. Jesus said, *"Do not think that I have come to abolish the Law or the Prophets. I have not come to abolish them but to fulfill them"* (Matthew 5:17 NIV). This means that we no longer have restrictions on the things we can eat. We can eat anything. This is what is written, *"Jesus declared all foods clean"* (Mark 7:19 NIV). *"Therefore, do not let anyone judge you by what you eat or drink"* (Colossians 2:16 NIV). And *"The kingdom of God is not a matter of eating and drinking, but of righteousness, peace and joy in the Holy Spirit"* (Romans 14:17 NIV). So these Ceremonial Laws relating to food were for the Jewish people.

When you read the Ceremonial Law, you will be surprised at how much blood was shed. Doves were killed. Lambs were killed. Rams were killed. Bulls were killed. Such an excessive amount of blood was shed because of sin. The Ceremonial Law made one thing clear, God cannot forgive sin unless the price of sin has been paid. In addition, all these sacrifices pointed forward in time to the coming of one person, the Messiah, who would be the lamb of God and would die for all sin, once for all.

---

[9] I am only giving a few examples of the 613 laws that governed Israel. For an example of instructions on the Tabernacle see Exodus 25–27, 30.

[10] For an example of priests' clothing and consecration see Exodus 28,29.

[11] For an example of dietary regulations see Leviticus 11.

[12] All Jewish males were required to attend three Festivals (1) The Passover – Leviticus 23:5–9, Deuteronomy 16:1–8, (2) The Feast of Harvest – Leviticus 23:9–22, Deuteronomy 16:9–12 and (3) the Feast of Tabernacles – Leviticus 25:33–42, Deuteronomy 16:13–15.

[13] For examples of laws on animal sacrifices see Leviticus 1, 4, 22:17–33.

The Bible says, *"Look, the Lamb of God, who takes away the sin of the world"* (John 1:29 NLT).

The Civil Law

The Civil Law governed the daily life of the Jewish people. It regulated things like property sales, property boundaries, marriage, divorce and workers' rights. It established a court system that issued sentences requiring restitution and punishments.[14] As an interesting note, did you know that there were no prisons in the Law of Moses? There was capital punishment. But, the Law of Moses focused instead on restitution, making right and paying back what you owed. The Civil Law cared for the poor and the foreigners who lived among the Jewish people.[15] God has always been concerned about the poor and foreigners. For example, farmers were instructed to leave the edges of their fields and not harvest them so that the poor could glean the unharvested portions for themselves.[16] Today, we are governed by the laws and court systems of the countries we live in and not Israel's Civil Laws. The Civil Law was for Israel in their day.

The Moral Law

The Moral Law revealed God's unchanging character. The Moral Law shows God's love, grace, patience, mercy, righteousness and justice. It establishes God's standard for you and me. God's standard means that He expects us to be perfect in our actions, thoughts and words. It also declares that we are not perfect and that, because of our sin and failure, God has the

---

[14] For examples of laws on (1) property see Leviticus 25:1–34, (2) marriage and divorce see Deuteronomy 24:1–5, (3) workers' rights see Exodus 21:1–11, (4) restitution see Exodus 21:12;22:15, (5) court system see Exodus 18.

[15] For examples of laws on treatment of foreigners see Exodus 22:21, Leviticus 19:33,34.

[16] For examples of laws regarding the poor see Leviticus 23:22; 25:35–55.

right to punish us. Most significant of all, the Moral Law proclaims that God Himself will provide a sacrifice for our sins. While the Ceremonial Law passed away after the death of Jesus and the Civil Law was for the Jews in their day, the Moral Law is for all people, of all time, no matter when or where we live.

Remember, a person is only made perfect in God's eyes by believing that God can do what He said He would do. Obeying the Law has never been the way to get to heaven. Let me share an example. God's Moral Law is like a mirror. If you look into the mirror it will show you what you look like, but it cannot do anything for you. The mirror will show you that your hair is out of place or that there is food on your face, but it cannot comb your hair or wipe the food off your face. Like a mirror, God's Moral Law shows us to be who we are, sinners. But, it cannot change us. The Bible says *"For no one can ever be made right with God by doing what the law commands. The law simply shows us how sinful we are"* (Romans 3:20 NLT).

The Law as a Lease Agreement

Let's go back in the story to the time when Israel left Egypt. Three months after leaving, they found themselves at Mount Sinai and there, God gave them all the laws and commandments through Moses. We read in Exodus 24 that when they received the Law from the Lord, the people agreed to be bound in a contract with God. They offered animal sacrifices and Moses splattered the blood from the sacrifices on the altar and on the people.[17] This contract became a binding lease agreement between Israel and the Lord. It is very important to understand this, so let me explain.

Remember, the Lord gave the land to Abraham, to Isaac and to Jacob and to their descendants forever. There is nothing that will ever change this. However, in the book of Exodus, Israel had burgeoned into a large nation. So, before taking

---

[17] See Exodus 24 for details.

possession of the land they entered into an agreement with God. They were going to be treated as tenants (Leviticus 25:23) on the land and this agreement determined whether or not they would thrive and prosper in the land or whether or not they would remain on the land at all. This is how the lease agreement read.

God said to the people that

> *if they obey all the commands, He would bless them.*
>
> *If they disobeyed the commands, He would curse or remove the blessings.*
>
> *If they continued to disobey the commands, He would remove them from the land.*

The nation of Israel understood the terms of the agreement, that God would respond to their obedience with blessings, to their disobedience with curses and finally, if they persisted, remove them from the land. So, they agreed to the terms by stating that they would obey.

> Then he took the Book of the Covenant and read it aloud to the people. Again they all responded, "We will do everything the LORD has commanded. We will obey" (Exodus 24:7 NLT).

This is the Old Covenant. From this point in time, the nation of Israel was under a binding lease agreement over the land. I will show you two passages that demonstrate how the Law was a lease agreement between God and Israel. The first is from Deuteronomy.

> Moses called all the people of Israel together and said, "Listen carefully, Israel. Hear the decrees and regulations I am giving you today, so you may learn them and obey them! The Lord our God made a covenant with us at Mount Sinai. The Lord did not

> make this covenant with our ancestors, but with all
> of us who are alive today" (Deuteronomy 5:1–3
> NLT).

Notice, the Old Covenant was different from the promises to the
patriarchs, who lived a few hundred years earlier. It was based
on obedience while the promise to the patriarchs was based on
faith.

> The Lord spoke these words to all of you assembled
> there at the foot of the mountain. (Deut. 5:22)

> So Moses told the people, "You must be careful to
> obey all the commands of the Lord your God,
> following his instructions in every detail. Stay on the
> path that the Lord your God has commanded you to
> follow. Then you will live long and prosperous lives
> in the land you are about to enter and occupy" (Deut.
> 5:32–33).

Another example is found in Leviticus 26. I want you to notice
the blessings, the curses (removal of the blessing) and the
removal of the people from the land if they persist in
disobedience. I am only going to highlight the main verses. But,
please take a moment and read the entire chapter.

Blessing

> If you follow my decrees and are careful to obey my
> commands, I will send you the seasonal rains. The
> land will then yield its crops, and the trees of the
> field will produce their fruit. Your threshing season
> will overlap with the grape harvest, and your grape
> harvest will overlap with the season of planting
> grain. You will eat your fill and live securely in your
> own land (Leviticus 26:3–5 NLT).

Blessing Removed (Curses)

However, if you do not listen to me or obey all these commands, and if you break my covenant by rejecting my decrees, treating my regulations with contempt, and refusing to obey my commands, I will punish you. I will bring sudden terrors upon you, wasting diseases and burning fevers that will cause your eyes to fail and your life to ebb away. You will plant your crops in vain because your enemies will eat them (Lev. 26:14-16).

People Removed from the land

I will scatter you among the nations and bring out my sword against you. Your land will become desolate, and your cities will lie in ruins (Lev. 26:33).

God Remembers His promise to the Patriarchs

But at last my people will confess their sins and the sins of their ancestors for betraying me and being hostile toward me. Then I will remember my covenant with Jacob and my covenant with Isaac and my covenant with Abraham, and I will remember the land (Lev. 26:40,42).

Notice, even though the people would be chased off the land for breaking the lease agreement, God would not forget the promises He made to the patriarchs or the land.

Old Covenant at Mount Sinai

These are the decrees, regulations, and instructions that the Lord gave through Moses on Mount Sinai as evidence of the relationship between himself and the Israelites (Lev. 26:46).

The words of Leviticus 26 were spoken by Moses as a reminder of the Old Covenant agreement that was made at Mount Sinai over the land. However, if you read the entire chapter you will notice that it also becomes a prophecy of what will take place over the next 1000 years after Moses died. It must have been heart breaking for Moses to realize that the people were indeed going to break the agreement and God would eventually keep His end of the agreement and remove them from the land.

Blessings and Curses from Gerizim and Ebal

God made the agreement with the people at Sinai in Exodus 24 and He kept referring to it throughout the books of Leviticus, Numbers and Deuteronomy. Then God asked the people to do something very interesting that would serve as a reminder of the lease agreement.

In Deuteronomy 11:26–32, Moses gave instructions that required the people to perform a ceremony as a way to reinforce this Old Testament agreement between them and God. As soon as they entered the promised land, they would find two small mountains called Mount Gerizim and Mount Ebal. These mountains stood opposite each other. Joshua was told to make an altar on Ebal and to carve the Law on the stones of the altar, while all the people of Israel watched him. Then, they were to divide into two groups with half of the people standing on Mount Gerizim and the other half on Mount Ebal. The tribe of Levi stood between the mountains and held the arc of the covenant. While Joshua read the entire Law, the people assembled on Gerizim were to shout the blessings for obedience and the people assembled on Ebal were to shout the curses for disobedience. In Joshua 8:30–35, we read that the people obeyed Moses' instructions and performed this ceremony under Joshua's leadership, soon after entering the land.

So the Old Covenant, which was a lease agreement, was made in Exodus 24. The people agreed to obey. God agreed to bless them if they did, to curse them if they did not and to remove them from the land if they continued to disobey. They were reminded over and over throughout the Law of Moses. And finally, they performed a ceremony to remind them of the agreement that they were bound to while living on this promised land.

Today, we live under a New Covenant. The New Covenant is the promise that whoever believes in Jesus the Messiah will be forgiven of all their sin and will receive the gift of the Holy Spirit. We first read this in Jeremiah 31:31–34.

A Prophecy about the Coming Messiah

Let's move away from this explanation about the Law and return to the main storyline of the Bible before finishing chapter three. There was a very significant prophecy made through Moses that reminded the people that a Messiah was coming to earth and that they should watch for this person. This is how Moses said it.

> The LORD your God will raise up for you a prophet like me from among your fellow Israelites. You must listen to him (Deuteronomy 18:15 NLT).

In the book of Acts, the apostle Peter quoted this prophecy and said that Jesus was this person Moses spoke of.

> Moses said, "The LORD your God will raise up for you a Prophet like me from among your own people. Listen carefully to everything he tells you." Then Moses said, "Anyone who will not listen to that Prophet will be completely cut off from God's people" (Acts 3:22 NLT).

CONCLUSION

Let's wrap it up. In the books of Exodus to Judges the storyline transitioned from the family of Abraham to the nation of Israel. We see that God kept His promise to Abraham by creating a nation from his descendants and giving the nation the promised land. In Exodus 24, three months after leaving Egypt, at the base of Mount Sinai, Israel entered into the Old Covenant. We witnessed the nation take possession of the land and receive the Law that governed their religious and civil life. We also learned how the Law determined whether the people were blessed or cursed or if they would remain on the land at all. In God's Law we see God's character. We see His expectation on our life, that we should be perfect. We see how imperfect we are. We also see God's provision of a sacrifice for sins. The sacrificing of lambs for sin, foretells that a person would come who is called the Messiah and He will be the one who suffers for our sin.

FINAL QUESTIONS

Q. Can you name the three purposes for God's Moral Law?

Q. How is the Law like a lease agreement between God and Israel?

Q. Why does the Bible say that believers are free to eat any food?

Q. In what chapter of the Bible is Old Covenant found? Can you remember when the Old Covenant was given?

CHAPTER FOUR

A Chosen Family – David

(Ruth, 1-2 Samuel, 1 Chronicles)

In case you didn't notice, we have been taken on a helicopter ride. I know helicopters did not exist back in the days of the Bible, but I like the analogy. What do I mean? Watch the way the story has been unfolding. We began by examining details about creation and one couple named Adam and Eve. But soon after, we hopped aboard a helicopter and were lifted up high in the air to gain an aerial view and see the larger story of the world filling with people. Then the helicopter landed and with our feet on the ground, we saw the details of one man Noah. After the flood, we boarded the helicopter again for a big picture view of people migrating across the earth. The helicopter landed again for us to get to know one person, Abraham, and his family. After this, the helicopter lifted off so we could see the aerial view of the nation of Israel settling in the promised land. However, when you read the book of Ruth, the helicopter has again set down, allowed us to disembark and learn about one person.

In the book of Ruth, our attention has once again been drawn from the national story to an individual woman. She lived in a land called Moab, which meant that she was not even Jewish. The fact that she is a Moabite is not a problem, but the story, since Genesis 12, has been about the Jewish people and God accomplishing His plan through them. So, why is the story focused on this Moabite woman? So far, there have been other women in the Bible, but why does this woman have an entire book dedicated to her? The answer is simple. We are being introduced to David. God has, once again, focused our attention on His promise to bring the Messiah into the world and He now reveals that the Messiah will come through the family of a man named David. This woman, Ruth, married a man from Israel named Boaz and became David's great–grandmother. Although the book of Ruth is only four chapters long, there is a prophecy spoken through the tribal elders and a short genealogy that connects David to Judah. This is what is written.

Elders Bless Ruth and Give a Prophecy

> Then the elders and all the people standing in the gate replied, "We are witnesses! May the Lord make this woman who is coming into your home like Rachel and Leah, from whom all the nation of Israel descended! May you prosper in Ephrathah and be famous in Bethlehem. And may the Lord give you descendants by this young woman who will be like those of our ancestor Perez, the son of Tamar and Judah" (Ruth 4:11,12 NLT).

Ruth in the Messiah's Line from Judah to David

> The neighbor women said, "Now at last Naomi has a son again!" And they named him Obed. He became the father of Jesse and the grandfather of David. This is the genealogical record of their ancestor Perez: Perez was the father of Hezron. Hezron was the father of Ram. Ram was the father of Amminadab. Amminadab was the father of Nahshon. Nahshon was the father of Salmon. Salmon was the father of Boaz. Boaz was the father of Obed. Obed was the father of Jesse. Jesse was the father of David (Ruth 4:17–22).

Through Ruth, David's ancestry is traced back to Perez, who was Judah's son. And through the story of Ruth's life we are given an example of how God includes all people in His plan. God chose the Jewish people to bring the Messiah into the world, yet He lets a woman who is not Jewish become part of the most important family line in history. His love and salvation are for all people.

The Word Messiah in the Bible

We began this study in Luke 24 by reading how three prophecies summarize the Bible's story and how they point to a person who would come into the world. This person is called the Messiah. Beginning with vague references to Eve's descendant, more detail was added as the story moved through the life of Abraham, the nation of Israel and now to Ruth's great grandson, David. But, from Genesis to Ruth, the word "Messiah" has not yet appeared in the text of Scripture. In fact, the first time the word Messiah appears in the Bible is in 1 Samuel 2:10. It is found in the most unlikely place, in the prayer of a woman named Hannah, the mother of the prophet Samuel.

The word Messiah means "anointed one." It comes from the Hebrew word Māshēakh (מָשִׁיחַ).[18] This is a masculine noun. There is another Hebrew word māshakh' (מָשַׁח). It is a verb that means "to anoint" or to smear oil on something. Anointing indicated that something was dedicated to God and uniquely set apart for Him. I admit that the word "anoint" appears in the Bible before 1 Samuel, but, only as a verb. For example, people smeared oil on priests, the tabernacle and some of the offerings.

---

[18] Messiah is a Hebrew word. Christ is a Greek word that means Messiah. So Jesus Christ means the same thing as Jesus the Messiah.

But, the Messiah, the anointed one, a person, is first mentioned in Hannah's prayer in 1 Samuel 2. This is her prayer.[19]

> The Lord will judge the ends of the earth. He will give strength to his king and exalt the horn of his anointed [his Messiah] (1 Samuel 2:10 NIV).

In her prayer, Hannah prophesied that the Messiah will be an exalted King who will judge the entire world. And, the Lord will strengthen the Messiah's kingdom. Interestingly, the second time the Messiah is mentioned in the Bible is in the same chapter. An anonymous prophet, who declared the demise of Eli's priestly family line, was aware that the Messiah already existed and that He would continue to live forever.

> I will raise up for myself a faithful priest, who shall do according to what is in my heart and in my mind. And I will build him a sure house, and he shall go in and out before my anointed [my Messiah] forever (1 Sam. 2:35 ESV).

This new priestly line will minister before the Messiah forever. Many believe that this priestly line is you and me who will be priests before God and the Messiah Jesus in heaven. What an amazing revelation tucked away in the prayer of Hannah. Samuel must have understood the meaning of his mother's prayer, because he twice asked the Messiah to bear witness to his innocence in 1 Samuel 12:3,5.

It bemuses me how God introduced something as important as the name "Messiah" through a single sentence of a prayer. It could be so easily overlooked. I know all scripture is God's word, but I must admit that I often consider verses like Hannah's prayer as throw away lines. I get absorbed in the

---

[19] For further study on the origins on the word Messiah see Walter C. Kaiser Jr., "The Messiah in the Old Testament," in Studies in Old Testament Biblical Theology (Grand Rapids: Zondervan Publishing House, 1995), 66-77.

amazing miracle of 1 Samuel 1 and consider 1 Samuel 2:1–10 as nothing more than Hannah expressing appreciation to God. We should pay close attention to all that is written. Think about this. Since Genesis 3:15, we were told that a person will come to earth to suffer and die for sins. But, now, through Hannah's prayer, we finally learn that He will be called the Messiah.

David's Son / God's Son

His title, Messiah, is only the beginning of revelation about this person. In this portion of the Bible another basic truth about the Messiah is introduced. He will be David's son and He will be God's Son. But, who is David? And what does the Bible mean when it says that the Messiah will be David's son and God's son?

David's Life Story

I like to think of the books of Ruth, 1,2 Samuel and 1 Chronicles as the story of David's life. Think about this. David was the second king of Israel and he was anointed king by an amazing prophet named Samuel. But, the book of Ruth introduces us to David before Samuel and before the first king of Israel, Saul. While 1 Samuel tells the life stories of Samuel and Saul, it also tells many of the highly acclaimed stories of David's life. It gives the account of how David was anointed king (1 Samuel 16), his victory over Goliath (1 Samuel 17) and of his frequent escapes from the murder attempts by a jealous king, Saul (1 Samuel 18,19). It would be safe to say that much of 1 Samuel is less about Saul and more about David waiting 15 years to be king. By the time we finally make it to 2 Samuel, the narrative breathes a sigh of relief that Saul was at last dead and the long anticipated kingdom of David could begin.

David lived about 3000 years ago. When we think about David, a number of famous stories are brought to mind, like his battle against Goliath or his adultery with Bathsheba and murder of Uriah (2 Samuel 11). However, among all the noteworthy events of David's life, one stands out as the most important of all. It is found in 2 Samuel 7 (also in 1 Chronicles 17). This story took place in one night. This night became the most important of David's life. On this night, God made promises to David like He did to Abraham. And the promises He made to David that night would unfold the rest of the Bible's story.

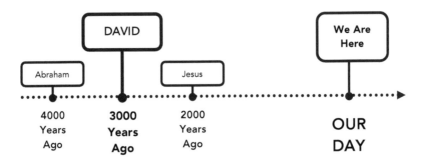

Timeline showing when David lived

By 2 Samuel 7, David had expanded Israel's borders far beyond what they had been up to that point in time. After this, he built a large house for himself that was made of cedar wood. As he went in and out from his house and he saw the Tabernacle, God's house, and he felt sorry for God. After all, the Tabernacle was a tent. There he was living in a magnificent house and God was living in a tent. So, David thought up an idea to build a gorgeous house for God. He told his plan to the prophet Nathan who not only liked the plan, but encouraged David to accomplish all that was in his heart.

That same night, however, the Lord spoke to Nathan and told him that He did not like David's idea. He asked Nathan to tell David that He had never complained to the leaders of Israel that He lived in a tent. Then the Lord instructed Nathan to tell David something that would become one of the cornerstone prophecies of the Old Testament. The Lord revealed to David that He would build David's house. This was the prophecy spoken to David.

> Now then, tell my servant David, "This is what the Lord Almighty says. I took you from the pasture, from tending the flock, and appointed you ruler over my people Israel. I have been with you wherever you have gone, and I have cut off all your enemies from before you. Now I will make your name great, like the names of the greatest men on earth (2 Samuel 7:8,9 NIV).

> The Lord declares to you that the Lord himself will establish a house for you. When your days are over and you rest with your ancestors, I will raise up your offspring to succeed you, your own flesh and blood, and I will establish his kingdom. He is the one who will build a house for my Name, and I will establish the throne of his kingdom forever. I will be his father, and he will be my son (2 Sam. 7:11–14).

> Your house and your kingdom will endure forever before me. Your throne will be established forever" (2 Sam. 7:16).

We learn two beautiful truths from these verses. First, God is the builder. It is He who fulfills His purposes for David. Notice how the Lord told David that He will establish David's house. I believe David's heart was very sincere and he wanted to do something wonderful for God. But the Lord was not interested in David's idea, no matter how sincere it was. It was not what David could do for the Lord, it was what the Lord wanted to do through David that mattered.

You and I are not David, but the principle is still the same. How often do we feel that we have a great plan and a sincere intention to accomplish something for God? We need to remember, like the Lord showed David, it is not our great ideas or what we can accomplish for God that matters. God wants to accomplish His work through us. David himself wrote, *"The Lord will fulfill his purpose for me"* (Psalm 138:8 ESV). You will experience real happiness when you realize that God is the builder of your life, your family and your work. All your good ideas may be sincere. But, God has a plan for you and He will fulfill his plan through you. Let Him lead.

Second, we learn that the Messiah will be the son of David and the Son of God. David was told that he will have a son whose kingdom will never end. This son will be a human descendant who will come from David's own family. In case you did not know, the Messiah is called the son of David (Matthew 22:42) and it is from 2 Samuel 7:12 that the term "son of David" is derived. However, 2 Samuel 7:14 also tells us that the Messiah will be God's Son. What does this mean? It means that that Messiah will be God. So from this text we learn that the Messiah will be both 100% man and 100% God. The importance of this night for David and for the story of the Bible cannot be understated. God, on this night, introduced something that we had not yet known about the Messiah.

Notice what takes place after this prophecy in 2 Samuel 7. As you continue to read through the Bible from this point on, David's name is mentioned over and over again. It was not simply that he was an important person and a great king. He is mentioned so much because God promised that the Messiah would come through his family line. Let me give you two examples. When Jesus was talking to the religious leaders of His day, He asked them a question. *"'What do you think about the Messiah? Whose son is He?' They replied, 'He is the son of David'"* (Matthew 22:42 NIV). In the last book of the Bible Jesus said, *"I am the root and the offspring of David"* (Revelation 22:16 NIV).

Before finishing this chapter, I want to pause for a moment and have you consider how important David and Abraham are. These men hold a very special place in the story of the Bible. Don't get me wrong. They were sinners like you and me. They needed a Savior like you and me. Just read the details of their lives as recorded in the Bible and you will agree, both Abraham and David were sinners who needed to be forgiven. While they were not superheroes, they both hold a very unique place in the story of the Bible. They are different because God made promises to these two men and the promises He made to them unfold the story of the Bible. Understand these promises and you will understand the story of the Bible. No other Bible characters had promises made to them like these two men.

I would like to show you a few examples so that you can see that the authors of the Bible were aware of Abraham and David's significance to the story of the Bible. The first example is written by the prophet Jeremiah about 400 to 450 years after David lived and 1400 to 1450 after Abraham lived.

> The Lord gave another message to Jeremiah. He said, "Have you noticed what people are saying? 'The Lord chose Judah and Israel and then abandoned them!' They are sneering and saying that Israel is not worthy to be counted as a nation. But this is what the Lord says. I would no more reject my people than I would change my laws that govern night and day, earth and sky. I will never abandon the descendants of Jacob or David, my servant, or change the plan that David's descendants will rule the descendants of Abraham, Isaac, and Jacob. Instead, I will restore them to their land and have mercy on them" (Jeremiah 33:23–26 NLT).

Another example is found in the book of Matthew. Have you ever noticed that the opening verses of the New Testament are a family tree? It is not exciting to read, but pay attention to which people are mentioned in the first verse of the New Testament. These words were written 1000 years after David lived and 2000 years after Abraham lived.

> This is the record of the ancestry of Jesus the Messiah, a descendant of David and Abraham (Matthew 1:1 NLT).

Another example is found in the story of the birth of Jesus. When the angel Gabriel appeared to Mary, listen to what he said.

> You will conceive and give birth to a son, and you will name him Jesus. He will be very great and will be called the Son of the Most High. The Lord God will give him the throne of his ancestor David. And he will reign over Jacob forever. His Kingdom will never end (Luke 1:31–33 NLT).

CONCLUSION

In Chapter Four, "A Chosen Family," our attention was drawn away from the large national story about Israel, away from conquering and dividing up land, to an obscure woman in Moab named Ruth. We see that her great grandson, David, became the king of Israel. But more than this, he would become as important as Abraham in the story of the Bible. He was promised a son and a kingdom. For the first time we are introduced to the person of the Messiah and we learn that this person is David's son and God's Son.

FINAL QUESTIONS

Q. Of all the Bible characters that could be named in Jeremiah 33:23–26, why does the prophet mention David and Abraham, Isaac and Jacob?

Q. Why does the New Testament begin with the genealogy of Jesus the Messiah (Matthew 1:1–17)?

Q. What is the Angel Gabriel's message to Mary in Luke 1:29–35?

Q. Mary was very young and not educated in religious schools. Do you think common people like Mary understood how Abraham and David fit into the story of the Bible?

Q. What does it mean when the Bible calls the Messiah David's Son and God's son?

CHAPTER FIVE

Poetry and Prophecy
(28 Old Testament Books)

Up to this point, the story of the Bible has been developing very slowly. Little by little, as years pass by, more detail is added. But now, with the main, foundational promises laid through Abraham and David, we enter a period in history when the flood gates of new information are opened. Suddenly, we pick up so much detail about the suffering of the Messiah, the Good News going to all people of the earth and the Messiah returning as a king, that it becomes a difficult task to summarize everything. On the following page, I have listed the books that are included in this chapter. They are broken down into four genres.[20]

Did you know that this chapter is by far the lengthiest section of the Bible? There are 28 books overviewed and it makes up 48% of the page count of the Scripture. There are many authors and they wrote over a 600–year period of time, from 1000 to 400 years before Jesus the Messiah came to earth. As you can see, this is a bulky portion of scripture and we are attempting to survey it in a few pages. To stay focused on the main story of the Bible, I have selected samples of verses to support what I am saying, but I will not be able to discuss them all. I would suggest that you take time to look up all the verses and let God's word convince you of what you need to learn.

---

[20] Job was probably written earlier than the other books included in this section. Also, I have included the historical books that pick up after the life of David in this chapter.

HISTORY BOOKS	POETRY BOOKS	MAJOR PROPHETS	MINOR PROPHETS
1 KINGS	JOB	ISAIAH	HOSEA
2 KINGS	PSALMS	JEREMIAH	JOEL
2 CHRONICLES	PROVERBS	LAMENTATIONS	AMOS
EZRA	ECCLESIASTES	EZEKIEL	OBADIAH
NEHEMIAH	SONG OF	DANIEL	JONAH
ESTHER	SONGS		MICAH
			NAHUM
			HABAKKUK
			ZEPHANIAH
			HAGGAI
			ZECHARIAH
			MALACHI

Books included in Poetry and Prophecy

Five Lessons from Poetry and Prophecy

From Poetry and Prophecy, we learn about 1) Israel – The Old Covenant and a future hope. 2) The Messiah will suffer and die. 3) The Good News will go to all people of the earth. 4) A New Covenant will be established. 5) The Messiah will be a King forever.

1. Israel – The Old Covenant and a Future Hope

These 28 books show us why Israel's history played out the way it did. So, let's take a moment to walk through what took place starting from the days of King David. David had a son named Solomon. Solomon had a son named Rehoboam who was next in line to be the king of Israel. However, under Solomon, there was a man named Jeroboam who was a city public works director. Jeroboam successfully led a revolt against Rehoboam and gained support from the ten tribes of Israel that lived in the northern regions of the country. The country divided and the ten tribes in the north who followed Jeroboam called themselves "Israel." The two remaining tribes, in the southern region of the country, followed Rehoboam and called themselves "Judah." The division between the north and the south took place around 931 years before Jesus the Messiah came to earth. The story is found in 1 Kings 12 and 2 Chronicles 10.

The books of 1 and 2 Kings trace the line of kings in both Israel and Judah. As for Israel, not one of their kings ever pleased the Lord and the blame for their rebellion against God was laid at the feet of Jeroboam (1 Kings 15:30). This is because Jeroboam, from Israel's inception in 931, introduced a counterfeit religious system as a way to drive a permanent wedge between the northern and southern kingdoms, keeping them from ever again reuniting as one (1 Kings 12:25–33). The counterfeit system included new centers of worship in Dan and Bethel to replace the temple in Jerusalem, a new priestly line to replace Levi, new gods in the form of 2 gold calves, a new story of the gold calves leading Israel out of Egypt and a new festival to coincide with and mimic the Festival of Shelters in Judah. In 1 and 2 Kings we read about the famous prophet Elijah and his protégé Elisha. They caused drought, called down fire from heaven, healed the sick and raised the dead in order to confront kings and show God's power to the people of Israel and Judah. Israel's demise, in 2 Kings 17, came at the hands of the Assyrians, who conquered and dispersed the people of the northern kingdom.

First and Second Chronicles narrate the story of Judah, the southern kingdom. They follow the family line of David from his son Solomon until the return from exile. This explains why the first nine chapters are genealogies, with 1 Chronicles 1:1–2:16; 3:1–24 tracing Adam to Abraham to David. Judah's kings oscillated back and forth from godly to evil. Sometimes a godly king was succeeded by an evil one and vice versa. Some kings started off well and turned away from God in their later years. Others started off evil and then turned to God with all their heart.

Divided Kingdom 931 BC

Ahijah prophesied that Jeroboam, a city publics work director under King Solomon, would divide the nation and rule over 10 tribes in the north (1 Kings 11:26–40). Rehoboam, Solomon's son, was king over the south. From 931, the nation was divided between a Northern and Southern Kingdom.

Eventually Judah was conquered and exiled to Babylon as recorded in 2 Chron. 36:17–21 and in 2 Kings 25.

As time passed by, both Israel and Judah forgot the Lord and disobeyed the Law. So, God sent prophets to call the people back to the Law. When you read the prophets, it might seem like they were critical and judgmental men with anger issues. But they were not. The purpose of the prophets was much more simple than this. Let me explain.

Do you remember the Old Covenant? Do you remember that it served as a lease agreement? God promised Israel that He would bless them if they obeyed, but He would remove the blessing and send curses if they disobeyed. And, if they continued to disobey, He would eventually remove them from the land.

So, the purpose of the prophets was very simple. They read the lease agreement. Then, they observed the behavior of the people and noticed they were disobeying the Lord their God. The natural consequence was for God to send curses and eventually remove the people from the land. So, the prophets spoke to the people warning them that God would fulfill His word if they continued to disobey. I will show you one example of this from Jeremiah.

The Lord reminded the people of the Old Covenant.

This is the word that came to Jeremiah from the Lord. "Listen to the terms of this covenant and tell them to the people of Judah and to those who live in Jerusalem. Tell them that this is what the Lord, the God of Israel, says. 'Cursed is the one who does not obey the terms of this covenant – the terms I commanded your ancestors when I brought them out of Egypt, out of the iron-smelting furnace.' I said, 'Obey me and do everything I command you, and you will be my people, and I will be your God. Then I will fulfill the oath I swore to your ancestors, to give them a land flowing with milk and honey' – the land you possess today" (Jeremiah 11:1–5 NIV).

Next, the Lord sent curses.

The Lord said to me, "Proclaim all these words in the towns of Judah and in the streets of Jerusalem. 'Listen to the terms of this covenant and follow them. From the time I brought your ancestors up from Egypt until today, I warned them again and again, saying, "Obey me." But they did not listen or pay attention. Instead, they followed the stubbornness of their evil hearts. So I brought on them all the curses of the covenant I had commanded them to follow but that they did not keep'" (Jeremiah 11:6–8).

Finally, the Lord removed the people from the land.

Therefore, the Lord Almighty says this. "Because you have not listened to my words, I will summon all the peoples of the north and my servant Nebuchadnezzar king of Babylon," declares the Lord, "and I will bring them against this land . . . This whole country will become a desolate wasteland, and these nations will serve the king of Babylon seventy years" (Jeremiah 25:8–9,11).

Before they were removed, the Lord foretold the name of the king that would carry them off into captivity, Nebuchadnezzar of Babylon.

As stated earlier, both Israel and Judah were eventually removed from the land. This took place in two stages and by two different nations, the Assyrians and the Babylonians. Both of these nations were located in present day Iraq. About 722 years before Jesus came to earth, the Assyrians invaded the northern tribes of Israel and took them away into captivity. Then, around

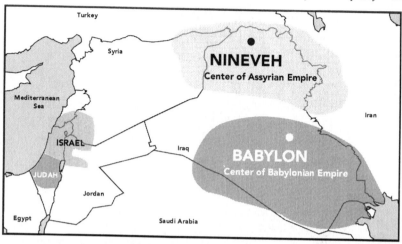

The centers of the Assyrian Kingdom in 722 BC and the Babylonian Kingdom in 586 BC are superimposed over a map of present day country boundaries. Both kingdoms were far larger at their pinnacles.

586 years before Jesus came to earth, The Babylonians invaded Judah and took them into captivity. So, we see that the Lord kept His word and honored His obligation in the lease agreement (The Old Covenant). He removed the people from the land because they disobeyed the Law.

What a sad ending. The people entered the land a few hundred years earlier, during the days of Joshua, with great hope of what the future would hold. Unlike any other nation on earth, they entered into an agreement with God that promised prosperity and blessing if they would simply walk with the Lord. This agreement was not answering the question of how the people would go to heaven. They would go to heaven because of faith and only because of faith in God's promise. But, their prosperity, peace and ability to remain on the land was dependent on their obedience. Tragic as this is, Israel's binding Old Covenant is proof that we as human beings naturally sin and turn away from God. Our obedience to God will always fall short of what God expects. We need God to save us. We need Him to rescue us from our sin and the outcome of our sinful lifestyle.

But, this is not the end of the story. The prophets also had a message of hope and restoration for the nation of Israel. Listen to what Jeremiah wrote.

> "The days are coming," declares the Lord, "when I will bring my people Israel and Judah back from captivity and restore them to the land I gave their ancestors to possess," says the Lord (Jeremiah 30:3 NIV).

> This is what the LORD says. "You will be in Babylon for seventy years. But then I will come and do for you all the good things I have promised, and I will bring you home again. For I know the plans I have for you," says the Lord. "They are plans for good and not for disaster, to give you a future and a hope" (Jeremiah 29:10,11 NLT).

There are many similar prophecies that predicted Israel's repatriation from Babylon to Israel. These two examples were written about 60 years before Israel returned from Babylon. It shows us that God is very compassionate. Although they were being carried away as captives, He encouraged them with a hopeful future. Around 538 years before Jesus came to earth, we see this prophecy being accomplished as Israel began to return to their land. The books of Nehemiah, Ezra, Haggai and Zechariah tell how the people returned in waves to rebuild the walls around Jerusalem and the temple that had been destroyed by the Babylonians.

Israel Scattered and Gathered

The prophets also wrote about another period in Israel's distant future, but this time they would be scattered among all the nations. This would take place many years after they had returned from their captivity in Babylon. Jeremiah wrote,

I will scatter them among the nations that neither they nor their ancestors have known (Jeremiah 16:9 NIV).

I will disperse you among the nations and scatter you through the countries (Ezekiel 22:15 NIV).

These prophecies were fulfilled after Jesus the Messiah suffered and died. The Jewish nation was dispersed from their land and many scholars point to the destruction of the Jewish temple in 70 AD as a major historical event that marked the end of the nation of Israel. Since that time the Jewish people have lived among other nations and in other lands. At times they have thrived and at times they have been persecuted. But, as the prophets predicted, they were indeed scattered among all the nations for nearly 2000 years.

The prophets also wrote about a time in the future, when God would gather together the Jewish people from all the nations where He had scattered them. He would bring them back to the land. Listen to what Jeremiah wrote.

"For I will bring them from the north and from the distant corners of the earth." Listen to this message from the LORD, you nations of the world. Proclaim it in distant coastlands. The LORD, who scattered his people, will gather them and watch over them as a shepherd does his flock (Jeremiah 31:8,10 NLT).

God began to fulfill this prophecy in 1948, when Israel became a nation again. And since 1948, He has continued to gather the scattered people of Israel back to the land that was promised to Abraham, Isaac and Jacob. Think about this. Two thousand five–hundred years before Israel returned in 1948, God said it would happen. It is only in recent history that God started returning the Jewish people to their land and the Bible tells us this is one of the signs that Jesus the Messiah is about to return as a king over the whole earth.

Do you remember the question that the apostles asked Jesus in Acts 1:6? They pressed Him to know, "Is this the time when You will restore the kingdom to Israel?" What do you think? Are the events taking place in our day in the land of Israel only political or are they prophetic? Is it all coincidence? Or is it God's timing?

Summary

We see prophecies made that Israel and Judah would be taken away to Assyria and Babylon and that they would be repatriated to the land of their patriarchs. This happened because God kept his word that if they disobeyed He would remove them from the land. Their return to the land allowed the Messiah to come to His nation and die on the cross. Second, we see a time foretold when Israel would be scattered among all the nations of the earth and a time when they would be returned to their land. Since Jewish people are returning to the land in our day, it is a sign that the Messiah will return very soon.

2. The Messiah Suffered and Died for Sin

On the following page you will find a chart that lists 25 prophecies. Three general observations can be made. First, the prophecies tell us a lot more than a few scant details surrounding the Messiah's death and resurrection. We also learn many essential facts about the Messiah's life. For example, we see the way He was born, the place He was born, the events surrounding His ministry, the place He would minister, the miracles He would perform, the way He would be betrayed, how a sword would pierce His side, how His clothes would be gambled away at His death, the place He would be buried – in a rich man's tomb – as well as His resurrection.

Second, notice how precise the prophecies are. They are not vague statements shrouded in mystical symbolism like those

PROPHECY ABOUT THE MESSIAH	OLD TESTAMENT Prophecy Written	NEW TESTAMENT Prophecy Fulfilled
Born in Bethlehem	730 BC Micah 5:2	Matthew 2:1
Born from a Virgin	700 BC Isaiah 7:14	Matthew 1:18
Many children killed	600 BC Jeremiah 31:15	Matthew 2:16
Spent time in Egypt	750 BC Hosea 11:1	Matthew 2:14
His ministry in Galilee	700 BC Isaiah 9:1-2	Matthew 4:12-16
He would heal the sick	700 BC Isaiah 35:5,6	Matthew 11:5,6
Enter Jerusalem on donkey	520 BC Zechariah 9:9	Luke 19:35
Rejected by his people	700 BC Isaiah 53:3	John 1:1
Betrayed by a close friend	1000 BC Psalm 41:9	Mark 14:10
Sold for 30 pieces of silver	520 BC Zechariah 11:12	Matthew 26:15
"Field of Blood" purchased	520 BC Zechariah 11:12	Matthew 26:6,7
Silent at His trial	700 BC Isaiah 53:7	Matthew 26:62,63
Mocked at His trial	1000 BC Psalm 22:6-8	Matthew 27:29,39,40
He will suffer & die for sin	700 BC Isaiah 53:4,5	Matthew 8:16,17
He will die for sinners	700 BC Isaiah 53:12	Matthew 27:38
His hands and feet pierced	1000 BC Psalm 22:16	John 20:27
He will drink vinegar	1000 BC Psalm 69:21	John 19:29
Pierced with a spear	520 BC Zechariah 12:10	John 19:34
His clothes gambled away	1000 BC Psalm 22:18	Mark 15:24
He will not break a bone	1000 BC Psalm 34:20	John 19:33
Died at an exact time	530 BC Daniel 9:25,26	Matthew 21:8–11
Buried with sinners	700 BC Isaiah 53:9	Matthew 27:57–60
Buried in rich man's tomb	700 BC Isaiah 53:9	Matthew 27:57–60
Resurrected on 3rd day	1000 BC Psalm 16:10	Matthew 28:9
Will ascend into heaven	1000 BC Psalm 68:18	Luke 24:50,51

in horoscopes, palm readings, magic cards or omens seen in animal livers. They are not general predictions that could come true for anyone. Bible prophecy is very precise and this is what makes it unique and true.

Third, notice that the prophecies are made many years in advance of the events. All of the prophecies listed in this chart were written between 1000 to 500 years before Jesus came to earth to suffer and die. Through these prophecies lots of information is revealed, with accurate precision, many years before the events. When it comes to prophecy, there is not another book like the Bible. When the true Messiah came to earth, He could be easily identified by the details revealed in the prophecies.

3. The Good News to All People of the Earth

In Poetry and Prophecy, we read prophecies about the Good News reaching every people group on earth. The hope and blessing that the Messiah brings was not limited to the Jewish people. It is for all people. That includes you and me. I am going to show you a few examples to demonstrate what I mean.

These words were spoken 1000 years before Jesus came to earth.

> May God be gracious to us and bless us and make his face shine on us. So that your ways may be known on earth, your salvation among all nations (Psalm 67:1–2 NIV).

> Sing to the Lord a new song. Sing to the Lord, all the earth. Sing to the Lord, praise his name. Proclaim his salvation day after day. Declare his glory among the nations, his marvelous deeds among all peoples (Psalm 96:1–2 NIV).

These words were written 700 years before Jesus came to earth.

Sing a new song to the LORD! Sing his praises from
the ends of the earth! Sing, all you who sail the
seas, all you who live in distant coastlands (Isaiah
42:10 NLT).

Let all the world look to me for salvation. For I am
God. There is no other (Isaiah 45:22 NIV).

I will also make you a light for the Gentiles, that my
salvation may reach to the ends of the earth (Isaiah
49:6 NIV).

Anyone reading this section of the Bible will be overwhelmed
with an abundance of evidence that God cares about all the
people of the earth. His care, His love, His salvation will reach
all people from every language. In these verses we hear happy
hearts singing praises to Israel's God. We hear voices daily
proclaiming salvation to listening ears. We see God's glory and
miracles being spread by word of mouth till they reach the ears
of all people groups on the earth. Sailors, island and city
dwellers, those who live in the mountains, in the plains and by
the sea are engulfed in the outpouring of God's salvation. The
prophets wrote of an unstoppable, global tidal wave of salvation
and God Himself is causing the surge. Not everyone will receive
the message, because not every heart is open to God. But many
will open their hearts and receive the blessing of Israel's
Messiah.

Think about this. God had his eye on you and me when He
gave these words to the prophets. When we believed in Jesus, it
was not a surprise to God. His salvation has reached you and me
exactly as He said it would. And, no matter how impossible it
may seem for the Good News to move across religious and
cultural boundaries today, we must remember that this prophecy
is guiding the events of our day. His salvation will cross any
boundary and reach people from all nations. These are the
greatest days to be alive, because we see these prophecies being

fulfilled in our time. God will fulfill His word. The apostle Peter said, *"Every prophet spoke about what is happening today"* (Acts 3:24 NLT).

4. A New Covenant

The Poetry and Prophecy books teach us about a New Covenant. We learn three truths about the New Covenant. First, it is new. Do you remember the Old Covenant in Exodus 24, the lease agreement at Mount Sinai? That was for the Jewish people. The New Covenant is for all people who believe in Jesus. This is what Jeremiah said about it.

> "The days are coming," declares the Lord, "when I will make a new covenant with the people of Israel and with the people of Judah. It will not be like the covenant I made with their ancestors when I took them by the hand to lead them out of Egypt, because they broke my covenant" (Jeremiah 31:31,32 NIV).

Second, we learn that the New Covenant is the gift of the Holy Spirit. Jeremiah wrote,

> "This is the covenant I will make with the people of Israel after that time," declares the Lord. "I will put my law in their minds and write it on their hearts. I will be their God, and they will be my people (Jeremiah 31:33 NIV).

> I will give you a new heart and put a new spirit in you. I will remove from you your heart of stone and give you a heart of flesh. And I will put my Spirit in you and move you to follow my decrees and be careful to keep my laws (Ezekiel 36:26,27 NIV).

Third, we learn that the New Covenant is for all people, not only the Jewish people. Joel the prophet wrote,

I will pour out my Spirit on all people (Joel 2:28 NIV).

5. The Messiah Returns as a King Forever

Finally, this section called Poetry and Prophecy writes extensively about the Messiah returning to be a king. These days are still in the future for us. Often, when we think about end times prophecy, we assume that most of it is written in the book of Revelation. While the book of Revelation does tell us about the future, most of what we know about the Messiah's coming kingdom, the Messianic Age and eternity, comes out of the section called Poetry and Prophecy. It is intriguing and even mystifying when we consider that the prophets who lived so many years ago, wrote about events and people that lie in the future. But, more than the many events and people, it is the one person, the Messiah, and the one event, His return as a king, that becomes center stage of the prophetic drama. What I am going to do at this point is make you wait until we get to chapter 8, "The Conclusion," to teach on the end times and future things.

CONCLUSION

Let's wrap up this chapter. With 28 books written over 600 years and almost 50% of the pages of the scripture, Poetry and Prophecy is the lengthiest portion of the story of the Bible. We have covered all of this very quickly. My goal has been to give you a lens to look through so that the next time you read these books, you will be able to keep the main purpose in view. We learn that the Old Covenant of Exodus 24 was pivotal in the way the history of Israel worked out and directly connected to the message of the prophets. We are given more detail about the Messiah's suffering and about the Good News going to all people than has been given so far in the Bible. We also read a message of hope for Israel that continues up to today. Remember, we will revisit this section in chapter 8 and examine many verses that relate to the future.

Think about it. This section of the Bible spells out in detail the three prophecies. This means that approximately 2400–3000 years ago, God announced what He would be accomplishing in our present day. History is not meandering aimlessly. God has destined that nations would come and go, but in the end, He would accomplish all that He said would happen. I realize that there are sections in the prophets that are very confusing. Who doesn't feel a bit puzzled by the metaphors and visions that are sprinkled throughout their writings. However, we should not come away from the prophets with a sense of bewilderment. We should understand the very clear statements made about the times we live in. We should be empowered by the prophecies that God is fulfilling in our day. Prophecy gives us a way to interpret history and to clarify the current events of our time.

FINAL QUESTIONS

Q. How does prophecy help us to interpret history?

Q. What is the possibility that any one person could fulfill all the prophecies that Jesus fulfilled?

Q. How does the Old Covenant help us to understand how Israel's history played out?

CHAPTER SIX

Jesus:

The Messiah Who Suffered

(Matthew, Mark, Luke, John)

Four hundred years elapsed between the last book of the Old Testament and the events of the New Testament. During this time, the Jewish people had returned and resettled in Israel and, in 63 BC, they came under the control of the Roman government. A number of religious and political sects had formed among the people – the Samaritans, the Pharisees, the Sadducees and the Herodians – all with differing agendas for the nation. Eventually, the exact time arrived and the stage was set for the Messiah to come to earth.

We know that the prophecies were given in the 39 books of the Old Testament and they were fulfilled in the 27 books of the New Testament. But, did you know that Daniel 9:24–27 foretold the exact time that the Messiah would come to earth and initiate the fulfillment of all three prophecies?[21] This is significant, because the New Testament writers wanted us to know that Jesus was the Messiah and that His appearance was perfectly timed to match Daniel's prediction. The apostle Paul wrote, *"When the right time came, God sent his Son, born of a woman"* (Galatians 4:4 NLT).

---

[21] See the chart that shows prophecies about Messiah's Suffering in Poetry and Prophecy. Some people believe that the prophecy in Daniel 9:24–27 predict the exact week, Passover Week, that Jesus would enter Jerusalem.

The first four books of the New Testament are called the Gospels. Gospel means Good News. The Gospels tell the life story of Jesus. He is the main character of the Bible and the Messiah that was promised to come to earth. In all four Gospels, the writers show us who Jesus was and what He did. They record details about Jesus birth, His life, His miracles, His teaching, His betrayal, trials, crucifixion and resurrection. They do this to show us that Jesus was both God and man, who lived a perfect life, offered Himself as a sacrifice for sins, defeated death, began a New Covenant in His blood, will return as the king and told His followers to go tell the Good News everywhere. This gives any reader the opportunity to match the details of Jesus' life with the prophecies made in the Old Testament and decide for themselves whether or not Jesus was the Messiah who was predicted to come? The verdict is quite overwhelming. He fulfills all the prophecies, leaving no space for coincidence.

10 Reasons – Jesus was the Messiah

For the remainder of this chapter, I will show you how the authors of the Gospels presented the case that Jesus was the Messiah.

1. Explicit Claims

The writers made explicit claims that Jesus was the Messiah.

> This is the genealogy of Jesus the Messiah, the son of David, the son of Abraham (Matthew 1:1 NIV).

> The beginning of the Good News about Jesus the Messiah, the Son of God (Mark 1:1 NIV).

> Many have undertaken to draw up an account of the things that have been fulfilled among us. Today, in

the town of David, a Savior has been born to you. He is the Messiah, the Lord (Luke 1:1, 2:11 NIV).

These things are written that you may believe that Jesus is the Messiah, the Son of God and that by believing you may have life in His name (John 20:31 NIV).

These explicit claims are helpful because they are unambiguous and straight forward statements from the writers about their understanding of who Jesus was. Next, let's look at the evidence the writers presented to validate their claims. The evidence aligns with Old Testament prophecy about the Messiah.

2. The Birth of Jesus

We learned from David's life that the Messiah is both God and man. But, there are many other verses in the Old Testament that also make this clear. For example, 700 years before Jesus came to earth, the prophet Isaiah wrote,

To us a child is born, to us a son is given. And the Government will be on His shoulders and His name will be called Wonderful Counselor, Mighty God, Everlasting Father, Prince of Peace (Isaiah 9:6 NIV).

In this verse, Isaiah stated that a male human being will be born whose name is Mighty God. This is one example of an Old Testament prophet predicting the Messiah will be both God and man. But next, I want you to notice that the apostles understood the prophets teaching about the Messiah and they too stated that Jesus was both God and man.

In the beginning was the Word and the Word was with God and the Word was God (John 1:1 NIV).

> The Word became flesh and made His dwelling
> among us (John 1:14 NIV).

The apostle John called Jesus "the Word." So, let's insert "Jesus" into the text, in place of "the Word." This is how it reads.

> In the beginning was Jesus and Jesus was with God
> and Jesus was God. Jesus became flesh and made
> His dwelling among us.

Put the statements together and we see that John proclaimed that Jesus was God who became a man and lived on earth among other human beings. Although He is God, Jesus has a unique identity as a separate person from the Father. This is about the simplest way that anyone could say it and it agrees with the prophets' teaching.

3. The Family Tree / Genealogy of Jesus

The genealogies also demonstrate that Jesus the Messiah was God and man. Matthew shows Jesus' human nature in a genealogy that connects Him to Abraham.

> This is the genealogy of Jesus the Messiah, the son
> of David, the son of Abraham (Matthew 1:1 NIV).

Luke connects Jesus' human ancestry to Adam. By doing so, Luke reminds us of the promise made to Eve, that from her family tree someone would come to crush the head of Satan.

> Jesus was known as the son of Joseph. Joseph was
> the son of Heli . . . the son of Adam (Luke 3:23–38
> NLT).

Jesus' human ancestry can be traced back to David, Abraham and Adam. But how is His ancestry connected to God? How can any person connect their family tree to God? The answer is found in the miracle of the virgin birth. Jesus had a mother. Her name was Mary. Mary, we are told, had not slept with any man, not even her fiancé Joseph. So, when she became pregnant with Jesus, it was a miracle from God.[22] But it was more than a miracle. This miracle established that Jesus was God. Notice the words that were spoken to Mary.

> The Holy Spirit will come upon you, and the power of the Most High will overshadow you. So the baby to be born will be holy, and he will be called the Son of God (Luke 1:35 NLT).

Many have tried to define what "overshadow" means, thinking that if we can decipher the meaning of the word, we will be able to offer a simple explanation for the virgin birth. But, the word overshadowed means overshadowed. It does not shed any additional light on the meaning. The conception was a miracle from God the Holy Spirit. However, we can say that the miracle means that God became a man. This happened so that Jesus' name could be called "the Son of God."

4. The Miracles of Jesus

Jesus healed, cast out demons and raised dead people to life because He felt compassion for them. But, He also performed miracles to demonstrate that He was the Messiah. Jesus taught that He was the Messiah. But, for those who would not take Him at His word alone, He invited them to witness His miracles and be convinced. Jesus said,

---

[22] The Bible does not teach that God slept with Mary and the result was a baby. That would be perverse. I have chatted with numerous people that have thought this is what the Bible teaches. They assumed that the Trinity is God the Father, God the Mother and God the Son. This is not the Trinity. This is not the Virgin Birth. This is not what the Bible teaches about God, Jesus or Mary. The Virgin Birth, according to the Bible, is the miracle surrounding how Mary conceived. It demonstrates that Jesus is God and man.

Believe in the evidence of the miraculous works I have done, even if you don't believe me. Then you will know and understand that the Father is in me, and I am in the Father (John 10:38 NLT).

Another example of this is in Mark 2:1–12. We read that Jesus healed a paralyzed man. The story shows us that Jesus was God with the power to forgive sins and heal the lame.

Now some teachers of the law were sitting there, thinking to themselves, "Why does this fellow talk like that? He's blaspheming! Who can forgive sins but God alone?" (Mark 2:6,7 NIV)

[Jesus said] "But I want you to know that the Son of Man has authority on earth to forgive sins." So he said to the man, "I tell you, get up, take your mat and go home" (Mark 2:10,11).

5. The Sinless Life of Jesus

The New Testament writers taught that Jesus lived a perfect life. He was tempted in every way just as we are, yet He never sinned (Hebrews 4:15). In fact, Jesus said this about His own life. *"Do not think that I have come to abolish the Law or the Prophets. I have not come to abolish them, but to fulfill them"* (Matthew 5:17 NIV). When Jesus said He fulfilled the Law, He meant that He never sinned. He lived a perfect life. Being perfect, it meant He was the first man to be completely accepted by God the Father because of His own good life. No error. No sin. He pleased the Father. When He offered His life to die for our sin, He was able to die as a perfect sacrifice. He did not die for His own sin, but for your sin and my sin. He died as the perfect lamb of God. Jesus, the accepted man, died for you and me, the unacceptable.

On two occasions in Jesus' life the skies parted and the voice of God the Father spoke from heaven telling Him, *"You are my Son, whom I love. With you I am well pleased"* (Matthew 3:17 NIV). The first time was at His baptism (Matthew 3:17; Mark 1:11; Luke 3:22) and the second was on the mountain when His appearance changed (Matthew 17:5; Mark 9:7; Luke 9:35). No prophet or teacher ever heard the Father speak these words of acceptance. Jesus was the only one.

6. The Suffering and Death of Jesus

As stated before, the Gospels show us that Jesus is the Messiah who would come to suffer and die for sins. His death on the cross was motivated by God's love and is the greatest expression of God's love. When Jesus died on the cross, God's justice and man's sin met in one place. God's justice was satisfied and our sins were paid for. Let me explain what I mean.

God loves you and He wants you to be in heaven with Him. But, He had a dilemma. He wanted to forgive your sins. But, He could not. He could not forgive your sin until the penalty for your sin was paid. This is how God's justice works. Once the requirement of His justice was met, He could then proceed to forgiving you and me. But, His justice must first be satisfied. This is what the Bible says.

> Without the shedding of blood, there is no forgiveness (Hebrews 9:22 NIV).

> Every violation and disobedience received its just punishment (Hebrews 2:2 NIV).

In the Law of Moses, lambs were offered as sacrifices for sin. The lamb would substitute for the life of a person. The person should die because of their sin, but the lamb died in the person's place. This is what happened. A person would bring a lamb to the temple as a sin offering. They would lay their hands on the lamb and God would allow that lamb to carry the sin of the individual (Leviticus 1:4; 3:1,8,12; 4:33). When the lamb died, it died in the person's place. It died, so that the person would not have to die. Since blood had been shed for the person's sin, God's justice was satisfied. God was now able to forgive the debt of sin. The Bible teaches that Jesus was God's lamb.

> Look, the lamb of God who takes away the sin of the world (John 1:29 NLT).

> He personally carried our sins in His body on the cross (1 Peter 2:24 NLT).

> Surely he took up our pain and bore our suffering, yet we considered him punished by God, stricken by him, and afflicted. But he was pierced for our transgressions, he was crushed for our iniquities. The punishment that brought us peace was on him and by his wounds we are healed. We all, like sheep, have gone astray, each of us has turned to our own way. And the Lord has laid on him the iniquity of us all (Isaiah 53:4–6 NIV).

> He was oppressed and afflicted, yet he did not open his mouth. He was led like a lamb to the slaughter and as a sheep before its shearers is silent, so he did not open his mouth. By oppression and judgment, he was taken away. Yet who of his generation protested? For he was cut off from the land of the living. For the transgression of my people he was punished (Isaiah 53:7,8 NIV).

> Yet it was the Lord's will to crush him and cause him to suffer. And though the Lord makes his life an offering for sin, he will see his offspring and prolong his days (Isaiah 53:10 NIV).

Jesus, a man, died in the place of mankind. It is not enough that a lamb died in the place of a man. Throughout history, all the lambs that were offered only reminded people that they were sinners. That is why they had to come back again and again and offer lambs. In addition, all the sin offerings reminded people that God would one day provide a lamb as a sacrifice to die for the sins of all people. When Jesus died, He died one time for all people so that all the sins of everyone who believes in Him will be taken away forever. When Jesus died on the cross we see God's greatest expression of love. The Bible says,

> This is real love. Not that we loved God, but that he loved us and sent his Son as a sacrifice to take away our sins (1 John 4:10 NLT).

We did not reach out to God. It was God who first reached out to us. God took steps towards us and did something for us that we could never do for ourselves. He paid the price of our sin. Because He loves us, He paid our debt on the cross. Now, because of the cross, you and I can be clean and perfect in God's eyes. According to the authors of the Bible, Jesus was the Messiah who suffered.

7. The Resurrection of Jesus

The Gospels also show us that Jesus came back to life. He is no longer dead. He is alive. He lives forever just exactly as the Prophets said would happen. When Jesus the Messiah came back to life, He conquered death and defeated our greatest enemy. Everyone, no matter where they are from in the world, will eventually lose to the enemy of death. But now, Jesus has taken away the power of death and offers life to anyone who believes. It is not only Jesus who will live forever, but we too will live forever. This is called eternal life. This is what the Bible says.

> Since the children have flesh and blood, he too shared in their humanity so that by his death he might break the power of him who holds the power of death – that is, the devil – and free those who all

their lives were held in slavery by their fear of death (Hebrews 2:14,15 NIV).

Jesus said, "Everyone who lives in me and believes in me will never ever die" (John 11:26 NLT).

Jesus said, "I tell you the truth, those who listen to my message and believe in God who sent me have eternal life. They will never be condemned for their sins, but they have already passed from death into life" (John 5:24 NLT).

Jesus the Messiah was raised to life in order to give us life.

8. Jesus and the New Covenant

The Gospels teach that Jesus the Messiah is the one who initiated the New Covenant. His blood purchased a new agreement between God and us. Let's compare the New with the Old Covenant. First, it is called a New Covenant because it is new. It means the Old Covenant from Exodus 24 is no longer valid. Second, the Old Covenant was between God and Israel. The New Covenant is for all people. Third, the Old Covenant was a lease agreement regarding the land. The New Covenant has nothing to do with land. It is a promise that God will forgive any person who believes that the sacrifice of Jesus has paid for their sin. Fourth, the Old Covenant was a two–way agreement between God and Israel and depended upon Israel's obedience. The New Covenant is based on faith. It is a one–way agreement where God promises to forgive sins and give the gift of the Holy Spirit to anyone who believes. There is no obligation to obey the Law. It is based on faith in God's ability to do what He said He would do. This is what Jesus said.

And he took a cup, and when he had given thanks he gave it to them, saying, "Drink of it, all of you, for this is my blood of the covenant, which is poured out for many for the forgiveness of sins" (Matthew 26:27,28 ESV).

In the same way also he took the cup, after supper, saying, "This cup is the new covenant in my blood. Do this, as often as you drink it, in remembrance of me." For every time you eat this bread and drink this cup, you are announcing the Lord's death until he comes again (1 Corinthians 11:25,26 ESV).

According to this Bible verse, there are two reasons why believers break bread and drink the cup. The first is to remember that the Lord's death is what initiated the New Covenant. The second is to proclaim the Lord's death until He returns.

9. Jesus Taught – Go to all Nations

The Gospels teach us that Jesus, before leaving the earth, instructed His disciples that they were entering a new era when the Good News would go all people. God always loved the world and since the days of Abraham had been promising that the Messiah would bring a blessing for all nations. In the Old Testament, people were invited to come and see what God had done (Psalm 66:5). But in the New Testament, we are told to go and tell all what God has done through the Messiah Jesus. The time had finally arrived. The benefits and blessings of Jesus' death and resurrection were now to reach the ears of every person. Jesus said,

All authority in heaven and on earth has been given to me. Go therefore and make disciples of all nations, baptizing them in the name of the Father and of the Son and of the Holy Spirit, teaching them to observe all that I have commanded you (Matthew 28:18–20 ESV).

In chapter 7, I will unpack this in more detail.

10. Jesus the Messiah is King

The Gospels teach us that Jesus was the Messiah who would return to earth to be a king forever. Here are a few examples.

> When the Son of Man comes in his glory, and all the angels with him, then he will sit on his glorious throne. (Matthew 25:31 ESV).

> They replied, "When you sit on your glorious throne, we want to sit in places of honor next to you, one on your right and the other on your left" (Mark 10:37).

> Jesus said to them, "Truly I tell you, at the renewal of all things, when the Son of Man sits on his glorious throne, you who have followed me will also sit on twelve thrones, judging the twelve tribes of Israel" (Matthew 19:28).

In chapter 8, we will examine a timeline and events surrounding the return of the Messiah as king forever.

Summary

These ten points summarize a thesis proposed by Matthew, Mark, Luke and John. The proposition is simple. Jesus was the person that all the scriptures wrote about. He was the Messiah. They recorded detailed evidence to support their claim. They laid this evidence out in a way that gives all individuals the opportunity to read and decide for themselves what they think. They even recorded testimonial evidence of people who believed. For example, Martha, the sister of Mary and Lazarus, said, "*I believe that you are the Messiah, the Son of God, who is to come into the world*" (John 11:27 NIV). Was Jesus the Messiah? If so, then believe in Him and you will find a new life.

CONCLUSION

I want to wrap up this section with a few questions. Does this story make sense to you? Do you believe that Jesus is the Messiah? Do you believe He suffered and died for your sin? Do you believe that He is the One who came back to life again and is the One who offers life to all? It is not enough to simply understand the facts about Jesus. Each one of us needs to make our own personal response. When we believe, we have life in His name. The result of belief is life. If you do believe, then you should open your heart to Him and receive Him. He does not ask you to make commitments to obey him. He asks you to receive life from Him. This is what the Bible says you must do.

> If you confess with your mouth that Jesus is Lord and believe in your heart that God raised him from the dead, you will be saved (Romans 10:9 ESV).

To receive eternal life, you can pray something as simple as this.

> *Jesus, I believe that you are the Messiah who died on the cross to pay for my sins. I believe you can make me clean and acceptable to God. I believe that you have the power to give me eternal life. Please give me a clean life. Let your blood wash me clean and make me acceptable to God the Father. Give me a new life that will last forever. Give me the gift of the Holy Spirit."*

If you have prayed this prayer, then you have responded by faith. You have reached out to God's hand and received the gift that He has offered you. His hand is also reaching out to you and He has given you the new life you have asked for. You have received the blessing of the Messiah Jesus. Four thousand years ago, God said you would receive this blessing. He told Abraham, *"All families on earth will be blessed through you"* (Genesis 12:3).

CHAPTER SEVEN

The Good News to All People
(Acts and the Letters)

I have often thought that if the story of the Bible were mine to write, I would move the plot along much more quickly. Think about it. Since the time Adam and Eve sinned, God began to make His plan known that someone would come into the world to defeat Satan. But as the centuries crept by, God was not in a hurry to reveal the story to us. It seems to have taken so long for the Messiah to finally show up and for the Good News to be propelled forward to all people. In my version of the story, I would have brought Jesus to earth in Genesis 4 and solved the problem immediately. Then, by Genesis chapter 5, I would make sure that the blessing of the Good News reached all people of the earth and that the eternal, utopian kingdom was established. My Bible would be about 5 or 6 chapters long. But God's story is much longer and it makes me wonder why.

Please understand, I am not saying God was wrong. I am not saying that I know better than God. It is just that my curious mind cannot resist wondering why God revealed His plan at such a leisurely pace? Why did He take such a long time to bring the Messiah to earth and to spread the blessing of the Good News to all people? One conclusion I have reached. God is much more patient than me. He calmly lets the drama unfold over many centuries so that His family includes many people from all over the world. Here is how the apostle Peter wrote it.

> The Lord isn't really being slow about his promise,
> as some people think. No, he is being patient for
> your sake. He does not want anyone to be destroyed,
> but wants everyone to repent (2 Peter 3:9 NLT).

His patience does not answer every question, but it does give me time to think about my own life. What I mean is this. If God were as impatient as me, the twentieth century would not have come and I would not have been born. But, because God is patient and centuries have passed, I have had the opportunity to live, to hear the story of the Bible and to become a part of His family. You too, because you are alive, have the opportunity to hear the message of the Messiah and to make a choice to become part of the story that God is telling about our generation. We become like Bible characters participating with God to see the second prophecy fulfilled. These are the greatest days to be alive. In spite of the evil that is taking place in our world, we are watching the Good News reach every corner of the earth. More than passive observers of God's work, each one of us is able to join God to bring the Good News to all people.

The Great Commission

Jesus the Messiah came to earth in God's perfect timing. He showed the apostles that the Old Testament prophecies foretold a new season in history when the Good News would go to all nations. He initiated this new season by thrusting them out into the world with a command. We call this command the "Great Commission." The word commission means that there is a delegation sent out under someone's authority to carry out an assignment. We are the delegation who work under Jesus' authority. Our assignment is to bring the blessing of Good News to all people. This is how the command reads in the Bible.

> All authority in heaven and on earth has been given
> to me. Therefore, go and make disciples of all

nations, baptizing them in the name of the Father and of the Son and of the Holy Spirit, and teaching them to obey everything I have commanded you. And surely I am with you always, to the very end of the age (Matthew 28:19,20 NIV).

Go into all the world and preach the gospel to all creation (Mark 16:15 NIV).

As the Father has sent me, I am sending you (John 20:31 NIV).

Ethnicity

Let's return to the point in time when Jesus left the earth to examine how and where the message initially spread and to understand what is happening with the Good News in our day. We'll do this by looking at culture, the power of the Spirit, the first 100 years and the last 40 years. To begin, I want to revisit the Bible verse that we started with.

He told them, "This is what is written. The Messiah will suffer and rise from the dead on the third day, and repentance for the forgiveness of sins will be preached in his name to all nations, beginning at Jerusalem" (Luke 24:46,47 NIV).

In this Bible verse, Jesus set in place a sequential order. First, the Messiah would suffer, then the Good News would be told in all nations. But, what did Jesus mean by "all nations." The word "nations" in the English language is the word "ethnos" in the Greek language.[23] The Greek word ethnos is where we get our word ethnicity. In the Bible, it is most often translated Gentiles (non–Jewish people), nations or people, as in people groups.

---

[23] The New Testament was originally written in the Greek language.

Seeing the word "nations" as ethnicity or people groups, clarifies what it really means to bring the Good News to all people.

God Recognizes Our Ethnicity

I want to show you three important points about ethnicity. First, this verse tells us that God recognizes our ethnicity. If you travel internationally, you carry a passport. A passport recognizes your nationality, but not your ethnicity. Your ethnicity is identified by your language, your accent, your facial features, your skin color, the cultural traditions that you practice, the food you eat, your traditional clothing, your traditional music, your sense of humor and even the land you live on. All of these make up your ethnic identity. God recognizes that all of us have an ethnic identity.

God Affirms Our Ethnicity

Second, God affirms our ethnic identity. Admittedly, there may be areas within our cultures that are evil that we wish would change. But, that is not what I mean when I say that God affirms our ethnic identity. I mean that God brings Good News to your people and my people. He does not condemn our ethnicity. We do not have to speak a different language to pray to Him or sing in a different language to sing to Him. He understands our languages. He understands our cultures. This is why the Bible is translated into as many languages as possible. God not only recognizes our culture, He affirms it.

This may sound simple enough, but it was a big problem for the people who first believed the Good News. You see, the majority of the first believers were Jewish. For them, there wasn't a problem being Jewish and believing. After all, the Old Testament was Jewish, the prophets were Jewish and the Messiah was Jewish. So, it only makes sense that they enjoyed their Jewish ways while following Jesus as the Messiah.

But then, something happened. The Good News crossed cultural boundaries and spread to people who were not Jewish. In fact, in Acts 11:19, we read about what took place in Antioch, the third largest city of the Roman Empire. Such large numbers of non–Jewish people believed in Jesus that for the first time, a majority of the believers were not from a Jewish background. How strange this must have been for Jewish believers to witness so many non–Jewish people understanding the message and embracing Jesus as the promised Messiah. It was foretold by the prophets. But naturally, questions arose. What should they do with these people who were not Jewish? How were they to be included into the community of people who believe? Did God expect all non–Jewish people to become Jewish? Two main solutions were proposed. Some required people to abandon their ethnicity and become Jewish. They aggressively persuaded the non–Jewish people to be circumcised, to follow the Law of Moses and to practice Jewish traditions. These people were strongly convinced that the Good News was a call for all people to leave behind their ethnicity and become Jewish.

The apostles also addressed this question. They unanimously disagreed with those who taught that the Good News was a call to become Jewish. Instead, they taught that all people are free to be who they are. We do not need to abandon our culture. From Acts chapters 11–15, you can read how the tension over this issue built up and how the apostles resolved it. In the book of Galatians, you can read very clear teaching on this topic. Thank God that this problem was resolved early on. It means you and I can be who we are and we do not need to reject our culture to become a believer in Jesus as the Messiah. God affirms our cultures. He loves our different cultures. He wants to see the Good News come into our individual lives and then to spread through our cultures.

God Changes Our Ethnic Perspective

Third, God changes our perspective of other cultures. What I mean is this. Our ethnicity defines who we are. So, we end up seeing the world as "us" and "them." The people who belong to our ethnic group are called "us" and the people who belong to other ethnic groups are called "them." Every language uses words to label "us" and "them." Even the Jewish people used the word "Gentile" to refer to non–Jewish people. It is not unusual to develop very strong boundaries and equally as strong feelings about "us" and "them." Also, it is very easy to identify an "us" and a "them." The music, cultural practices and language, to mention a few, become very clear markers that draw lines between our culture and other people's culture. Sometimes, we even develop a hatred for those who do not belong to our group.

But, God changes our view of others when He moves into our lives. He helps us to see others the way that He sees them. He changes our desires so that we want to bring the Good News across the boundaries of culture and language to other people who are not like us. He changes our interests so that we want other people, from other cultures to experience the blessing of the Messiah, the same way that our culture has experienced His blessing. It is not a sin to love and enjoy our own culture and we will always identify with the culture we were raised in. But, God moves us to partner with Him and fulfill the second prophecy to bring the Good News across cultures. This process goes on until all people, in every corner of the world have been reached with the Good News. The Bible says.

> For you were slaughtered and your blood has ransomed people for God from every tribe and language and people and nation. And you have caused them to become a Kingdom of priests for our God. And they will reign on the earth (Revelation 5:9,10 NLT).

The Power of the Spirit

There is another problem. By nature, you and I are lazy and cowards. We are often too indifferent or fearful to tell the Good News to our own people, let alone other people who speak a different language and have a different culture. So when it comes to sharing the Good News, we feel afraid. How do we get over our fear and laziness and accomplish the job of bringing the Good News to all nations?

The answer is found in the person of the Holy Spirit. All of us receive the Holy Spirit at the moment we first believe in Jesus as the Messiah (Ephesians 1:13). He will never leave us (Hebrews 13:5). The Spirit brings joy, gentleness, healing and comfort (Galatians 5:22,23). But, the Spirit also brings power. The Bible calls this power "dynamite–explosive power" (Acts 1:8). The Holy Spirit replaces our apathy and fear with His desire and power, so we can tell the Good News. We need His power to do the job. The Bible says,

> You will receive power when the Holy Spirit comes upon you and you will be my witnesses, telling people about me everywhere in Jerusalem throughout Judea and Samaria and to the ends of the earth (Acts 1:8 NLT).

The First 100 Years

How well do you think the believers did during the first 100 years? Did they get on with the job and spread the Good News across cultural boundaries or did they fail? Jesus told them to go and gave them the Holy Spirit so they would have power and courage. But, how well did they do? A quick look at the first 100 years shows us that they made great progress spreading the Good News. Let's begin with the New Testament believers.

There are 27 books in the New Testament and, as stated earlier, the first four are the life story of Jesus. The fifth book is called Acts or the Acts of the Apostles. In this book we see the first thirty years of the advance of the Good News. The next 21 books are called "Epistles" which means letters. These books answer questions, give instructions, encouragements, warnings, truths and fill in some historical detail about the community of believers. The Epistles cover an additional thirty years of church history. So altogether, we get the first sixty years of history of the Good News from Acts and the Epistles.

Using the historical record found in the New Testament books we can trace the growth of the Good News. We see that it began in Jerusalem, went into Judea, Samaria and finally moved up into Antioch, a city in present day Turkey. The rapid growth of the church in Antioch resulted in a shift in the center of church activity from Jerusalem up to Antioch, with missionaries sent from Antioch to spread the message to many places around the world. The Good News also spread into Ethiopia, through all of Turkey, Greece, Rome and Spain. Adding traditions to the biblical account, we learn that the Good news spread into Egypt and across North Africa, into Armenia, Azerbaijan, Russia, Ukraine, Iran, Iraq and India.[24] This brings us up to the end of the first century.

The Good News Today

Church history, from the first century up to today, is lengthy, complicated and therefore, too much to discuss here. So, what I want to do next is skip from the first century to the present–day and give an indication of where the Gospel is spreading. First, while there have been pockets of Christian communities scattered around the earth for many centuries, growth seemed stagnant with only small missionary movements of any significance to be accounted for. For the past five hundred years, Christianity has mostly been considered a religion of Western

---

[24] Some church traditions are more easily confirmed than others. I have attempted to be judicious with church traditions and build a brief account based on those that are widely accepted.

countries. Although, this is not necessarily true. But, due to 200 years of missionary efforts, there has been a shift in the center of gravity. Since, the 1970s there have been more believers in Asia than in the west. And since the 1990s there are more missionaries being sent from Asian countries than from the western countries.

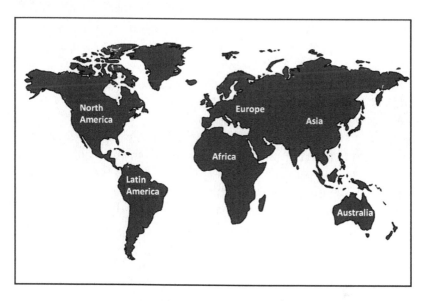

Latin America, Africa and Asia – the new centers of Christian Faith

Another way that some have analyzed the shift in trends and Christian populations since the 1970s is through what is defined as the "Global South." The Global South includes most of the countries of Latin America, Africa and Asia. It is where the largest portion of believers in Jesus are found in the world. And, from these regions, there are more missionaries sent to reach the unreached than anywhere else in the world. Paradoxically, while the Global South contains the largest portion of believers and sends the most missionaries, it also hosts the largest numbers of unreached people on earth. Unreached people are defined as people groups who have little or no access to the Good News, to Bibles or to Bible teaching.

To see the Good News reach all people, we need to create access. That is, we need to answer the questions of how to make the Good News, Bibles and Bible teaching more accessible to these people groups so that they are able to hear about the Messiah Jesus and His blessing. I want to give you some statistics from the International Mission Board (IMB). You can find these at imb.org. According to the IMB, there are about 200 million people who are unengaged and unreached. This means they have no access to the Gospel. There are four billion people who are engaged yet unreached. This means that they have some limited access to the Gospel. Then there are another three billion people that are considered no longer unreached. This means they have ample access to the Gospel.

Let me clarify this. At present, I live in the southeastern United States. There are people who live in this region of the country who do not believe that Jesus is the Messiah of Israel. These people are often referred to as "lost." So, we can say that there are lost people here and everywhere. However, the southeastern United States is reached. What do I mean? Any person living in this region of America has ample access to the Good News, to Bibles and to Bible teaching. So, while there are lost people all over the world, there are regions in the world that have very little opportunity, or no opportunity, to reach out and receive the blessing of the Messiah.

As believers in Jesus, our primary service is to create greater access for our fellow human beings to receive the blessing of the Messiah. Four thousand years ago, through the prophecy made to Abraham in Genesis 12:3, God declared that all people on earth would be blessed by Israel's Messiah. This should give us great confidence to realize that no person, no government and no demonic power can resist God's purposes. It should encourage us to stop focusing on the evil in our day and start looking to what God is doing. He is fulfilling an ancient prophecy before our eyes. However, we cannot sit passively and do nothing. We cannot drop our responsibility and place the burden solely on God's shoulders. We must realize that we are partners with God. We have been commanded by Jesus to go into all the world and make disciples.

Five Reasons We Do Not Go

I would like to point out five main reasons why most people have not become partners with God and have not invested their entire life into the work of the Good News. The first is ignorance. Some people are not aware that God has asked them to be a partner in His business. This usually comes from the teachers that influence them. Some teachers focus on personal wellness, psychological wellness or argue over whose doctrine is the most correct. These teachers have replaced the main story of the Bible as Jesus and the apostles told it with issues of lesser importance. Consequently, people under these teachers never see the central position of the three prophecies and they do not know that they are supposed to be partners with God to fulfill the prophecy of the Good News to all nations. When they hear teaching that highlights the main storyline of the Bible, they experience an awakening. For them, it is the first time that the Bible has been assembled in a proper order. For the first time, they are able to differentiate between the Bible's major teaching and its minor teaching. They have what I call an "Ah Ha" moment. "Ah Ha" they say. "Now I see." Is this you?

The second reason is that many people are preoccupied with living life. Life is busy. Work responsibilities, raising kids, extended family obligations, house repairs, etc., leave us with little time to think about anything else. We don't have any more time or energy to add one more thing to our life. If this is you, there may be a need to reevaluate your priorities and amend your lifestyle. I have raised three children and I know that when the kids are young you can feel overwhelmingly exhausted. So, sometimes it is impossible to avoid the business and we should not be too harsh on ourselves. But, if your life is too busy, because you have over committed yourself, I would suggest that you reprioritize so you can partner with God. You don't want to miss out on the experience of God working through you to fulfill His purposes in the world.

The third reason is boredom and laziness. For some of us, we have heard this teaching before, but it just does not move us anymore. We have become so familiar with it that we could teach it. But, there is no more passion within our soul, no more ambition or interest. We are not turned off by the Bible's main story, but neither are we turned on by it. It no longer lights our fire. If this is you, I would suggest two things. One is to ask God for renewed interest. Two, consider what it means to endure. Serving the Lord for the long run means owning up to the fact that every day is not going to be filled with excitement. We should ask God for grace to endure, even when life is boring.

The fourth reason is injury. I know a number of people who were completely invested in the work of cross–cultural missions, but were terribly hurt by other believers. As a result, they have dropped out of the work. Sadly, they have sacrificed careers, family, friends and years of their life to bring the Good News to other people. They have gained incredible skills, experience, speak other languages and understand how to minister to people who are from cultures different to theirs. But, as a result of being deeply hurt, they are on the sidelines, nursing their wounds and healing up. If you want to invest your life in the Good News, be prepared to suffer. At times it is painful beyond description, especially when the source of suffering is from those who should be loving and supporting you. I have no simple antidotes for those who hurt. Only prayer for restoration. All things are possible. *"He restores my soul"* (Psalm 23:3 ESV).

The fifth reason is paralysis. For some of us, we see the increase of evil in our world and we become paralyzed by fear. We begin to accept the story of conspiracy theorists and fear mongers who want to convince us that the entire planet is heading down the road to disaster. Fear grips us and we change our stance. We believe their dark teaching and, moved with a deep sense of foreboding, feel the need to defend ourselves from impending doom. We stock pile food in case the shops close and huddle together with other people who see things the way we do. Convinced that we need to escape the evil in the world, we barricade ourselves and batten down the hatches to protect all that we hold dear.

You might be thinking, "Wait a minute. Doesn't the book of Revelation teach that things get worse before the Lord returns?" My answer is, "Yes." I agree. Evil is on the rise and we should expect this pattern to continue. That is not the problem. The problem lies in the story spun by the conspiracy theorists and fear mongers. I believe they prey on people's minds by picking up on apocalyptic themes from the Bible and linking them with current events. Their goal is to generate fear instead of inspire faith. By creating fear, they create paralysis. Fear is what keeps their books selling and their radio programs on the air. It is a market. It is big business. And those who listen and subscribe to their story, become addicted to the fear and inactive in missionary activity.

When I read the Bible, I have not yet found a single verse where Jesus commands us to "Retreat! Run! Hide! Stock pile supplies! Preserve everything that you hold dear!" Jesus commands us to "Go!" There is no fear in His message. For those who are struck by paralysis, you need to consider how to throw off your fear and inactivity and ask for a fresh experience of the Holy Spirit so that you will be empowered with fearless faith.

Put yourself in the apostles' sandals. They had every reason to be paralyzed by fear. As they prepared to go, they knew that telling the Good News under Jesus' authority meant facing charges of treason against the Roman government. They knew the Jewish religious leaders would throw them out of the Temple and the synagogues and ultimately ostracize them from their own community. Going across cultural boundaries meant they risked being falsely accused of cultural insensitivity, racism or cultural imperialism. In spite of the potential for harm and mischaracterization, they accepted the risk, received the power of the Holy Spirit and spoke with unbelievable boldness. Here is an example of the apostles' response when they were told to stop spreading the story of the Good News.

> So they called the apostles back in and commanded them never again to speak or teach in the name of Jesus.
>
> But Peter and John replied, "Do you think God wants us to obey you rather than him? We cannot stop telling about everything we have seen and heard" (Acts 4:18–20 NLT).

CONCLUSION

Let's wrap it up. There is a need for people to leave their own culture and live among others with the goal of telling the Good News and teaching the Bible. There is a need for others to financially support those who go. There is a need for others to pray for those who go and to pray for the unreached to be reached. Just because you are not a missionary who leaves everything and lives in another culture, you can still reach the unreached who live near you. All of us have a part to play.

In your hometown, for example, no matter where you live, there are people residing near you from regions in the world that have little to no access to the Good News. God has brought them to live near you so that you can reach out to them. They might be a student or a business person. They might only be living near you for a short time. They might be settling permanently. But, they live near you. And God has sent them to live near you so they can be reached. Our world has become very mobile and people are on the move. Take your time with others. Reach out to them. These are the most exciting times to be alive. God is fulfilling this second prophecy and the Good News is reaching people from every ethnic group on earth. What will your part be?

FINAL QUESTIONS

Q. Have you ever considered using Operation World (www.operationworld.org) or The Joshua Project (www.joshuaproject.net) to guide your prayer for unreached people?

Q. How much time is built into your daily prayers for unreached people?

Q. Will you ask some of your friends to join you and pray the following prayer ?

My loving Father, thank you for letting me know the blessing of Jesus, the Messiah of Israel. Thank you for letting me experience your saving power and love. I give everything I am to you. I surrender all I have to you. Do anything with my life that needs to take place. Take away all my fears, for I know that you will do what is best with me. Make me someone who brings this blessing to others who do not know you. I want to partner with you and fulfill the Bible's prophecy by bringing the Good News to all people.

CHAPTER EIGHT

Jesus The Messiah is King

(Revelation, Future Prophecy, The Conclusion)

In chapter 8, we will study the conclusion of the story of the Bible. For many people, this is the most exciting part because it looks into the future. Every one of us is curious about the direction the world is heading, of what will become of our lives and what will happen after we die. So, this chapter ties together several topics and presents a timeline to overview how the future unfolds. I admit that the title is misleading, because the story of the Bible has no conclusion. It reaches into the future and continues on forever. But, we have one more book of the Bible remaining and this chapter sums up the visions and words of the final prophecy that the Messiah will return as a king forever. By the way, one final reminder, we are studying the story of the Bible as Jesus and the apostles told it. This means we are tracing the three prophecies that Jesus used to summarize the entire story of the Bible. First, a Messiah would come into the world to suffer and die. Second, the Good News would reach all people of the earth and third, the Messiah would return to be a king forever.

End Times and Bible Prophecy

As we turn our attention to the last of the three prophecies, we enter into an area of study called the "end times" or "eschatology." So far, we have covered every book of the Bible except one, the book of Revelation. When we consider the future, we might assume that the book of Revelation is the only book that addresses the end times. But, did you know that God has revealed details about the future in the books of Matthew, Mark, Luke, 1 Corinthians, Philippians, 1 and 2 Thessalonians, 1 Timothy, 1 and 2 Peter and Jude? And, did you know that most of what we know about the future comes from the Old Testament Prophets? So, in chapter 8, we are going to skim through a lot of Scripture.

As we read through the Bible and begin to piece together the events of the future, we must admit that we do not know everything. In fact, many fine points of prophecy are unclear. For some, this results in heated debates. But, I want to avoid debates. We should know that God's intention for telling us the future is to encourage and warn, not to inform us on every minute detail of every event. The warning is for those who do not believe that Jesus is the Messiah. If this is you, God wants you to turn to Him while He is patient. God wants you to believe and be rescued from the coming judgment, while there is time to soften your heart. The encouraging side of prophecy is for those of us who believe. Our reward is coming soon. Soon our trials will be over. We will receive new resurrection bodies and be with the Lord Jesus forever.

Sometimes the Bible makes very precise statements about people, nations and future events. At other times it makes vague statements that are meant to provide a rough description and set a general tone. When the Bible is vague, we should be content with the broad, imprecise meaning. When the Bible is precise, we can enjoy knowing the details God has given. Then, by bringing together the vague and the precise statements, we can paint a picture of the future. This enables us to connect current world events with prophecies about the return of the Messiah and make sense of our present day.

Bible prophecy is intriguing and it arouses our curiosity about the timing and circumstances surrounding events. Even the prophets examined their own writings.[25] I say this because some people shy away from talking about Bible prophecy, believing that it is all human speculation and conspiracy theories. I intend to avoid two extremes. On one hand, I do not want to read my own ideas into the text and create meanings that do not exist in the prophecies. On the other hand, I want to avoid scoffing at Bible prophecy as confusing, metaphorical literature that no one can understand. We can make sense of it.

Although, we do not know everything about the future, one thing you will notice, the tone of Bible prophecy is confident. Bible prophecy tells the future with certainty, as though it will happen, 100% for sure, no doubt. In fact, Bible prophecy is often written in past tense language, as though the events have already taken place. This is what makes Bible prophecy so alluring. Every detail is not clarified, but the bold assertive writing style reassures us the events will take place.

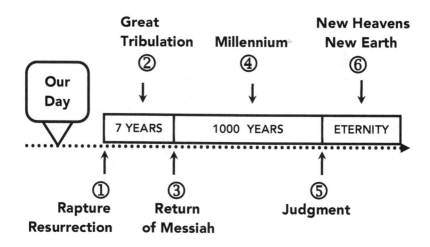

Timeline of Future Events

Six Future Events

In this next section, I would like to highlight six future events. They have been placed on a timeline above to show the sequential order. The six events are 1) the resurrection of the church, which some call the Rapture, 2) the Great Tribulation, which lasts for seven years, 3) the return of the Messiah as a king, 4) the Millennium or the Messianic Age that lasts for 1000 years, 5) The Great White Throne Judgment and 6) The New Heavens and New Earth.

(1) The Resurrection (2) The Great Tribulation

Every believer in Jesus needs to understand one important truth. The next big event in the future will be the resurrection of all who have believed. Some call this the Rapture, but the word that the Bible most often uses is resurrection. What does the resurrection mean and what takes place at the resurrection? First, the resurrection means that when Jesus returns, we will receive a new body. The Bible teaches that those of us who are alive when Jesus the Messiah comes back to earth, will be changed in a moment. We will not experience death, but we will be immediately transformed. Our body will be changed from its present condition, into a body that will not be affected by sin and will never die. The people who have believed in Jesus as the Messiah, but died, will come back to life. Their bodies will be raised out of the grave and they too will receive a new, resurrection body.

The two Bible texts that teach on the resurrection are 1 Corinthians 15:50–58 and 1 Thessalonians 4:13–5:11. We learn that Jesus will return in the clouds. He will call the dead believers back to life. They will immediately receive a resurrection body and will meet Him in the clouds. They go first. Then, we who believe and are alive on earth will follow them. We will automatically receive a resurrection body and fly up into the clouds to meet the Lord. The Bible calls this event the "blessed hope." This means that the return of Jesus the Messiah is a happy expectation. Why a blessed hope? Because we will receive a new resurrection body and we will see the Lord. We will be with Him forever. This is what the Bible says.

> But let me reveal to you a wonderful secret. We will not all die, but we will all be transformed! It will happen in a moment, in the blink of an eye, when the last trumpet is blown. For when the trumpet sounds, those who have died will be raised to live forever. And we who are living will also be transformed. For our dying bodies must be transformed into bodies that will never die. Our mortal bodies must be transformed into immortal bodies (1 Corinthians 15:51–53 NLT).

> For the Lord himself will come down from heaven with a commanding shout, with the voice of the archangel, and with the trumpet call of God. First, the believers who have died will rise from their graves. Then, together with them, we who are still alive and remain on the earth will be caught up in the clouds to meet the Lord in the air. Then we will be with the Lord forever. So encourage each other with these words (1 Thessalonians 4:16–18 NLT).

The resurrection body is a mystery and we do not completely understand it. But, let me give you a few helpful points about the resurrection body. First, the Bible tells us that Jesus' resurrection body is the prototype and gives us an example of what our resurrection body will be like (1 Corinthians 15:45–49). In His resurrection body, Jesus was recognized. He walked, talked and ate. He was touched and hugged. These are all qualities and activities that we do in our earthly bodies. But, He disappeared and reappeared. He flew and He could also make Himself unrecognizable or incognito. We cannot do this in our earthly bodies. When Jesus appears, we will be like Him.

> Dear friends, now we are children of God, and what
> we will be has not yet been made known. But we
> know that when Christ appears, we shall be like
> him, for we shall see him as he is (1 John 3:2 NIV).

Second, let me clarify a few misunderstandings about the resurrection body. We will not be spirits that wander without bodies (2 Corinthians 5:1–5). We will not be married (Matthew 22:30). We will not be reincarnated (Hebrews 9:27). Reincarnation teaches that the body is a shell that houses the soul and spirit. After one life, the body is shed off and the spirit and soul return to earth to find another body. The hope of reincarnation is to be released from the endless recycling of new bodies. The Bible does not teach reincarnation. It teaches resurrection. Resurrection is very different to reincarnation. Resurrection means that your body is yours forever. Your spirit, soul and body are what make your identity unique. At death your body decays back to dust. At the resurrection, the Lord raises your body back from the dust and reunites it with your spirit and soul. The resurrected body is your old body, raised from dust and changed into a new body that will never die. The Bible says, *"Many of those whose bodies lie dead and buried will rise up, some to everlasting life and some to shame and everlasting disgrace"* (Daniel 12:2).

Third, we are taught several truths about the resurrection body. It will be a spirit body with a different kind of skin. It will not have blood. It will not have any disabilities. It will not decay. It will not be affected by sin and it will not die (1 Corinthians 15:35–57). This means that from bowed legs and dyslexia to severe deformities of the body and mind, every human being will be released from the imperfections of the earthly body and will experience their body in its total perfection. It means that the inevitable results of decay, like rotting teeth, hair loss, osteoporosis and dementia, will never deteriorate and overcome our resurrection bodies. This new body will live on and on without ever ending. What I have briefly mentioned here is worth pondering. Have some fun. Imagine what it will be like.[26]

When Does Jesus Return?

There are three common views on when Jesus returns. Some say that Jesus returns at the beginning of the Great Tribulation and this is what marks the launch of the seven–year time of trouble. Some say that Jesus returns in the middle of the Great Tribulation and this is what marks a transition in the middle of the seven years, from 3 1/2 years of peace to 3 1/2 years of war. Some say that the church is resurrected at the end of the Great Tribulation and this is what marks the end of the age and the beginning of the 1000–year Messianic Age. I believe that the resurrection of the church takes place at the beginning of the seven years of the Great Tribulation. Jesus said that no one knows the exact day or hour when He will return (Mark 13:32).

In any case, every believer agrees that the resurrection of the believers means that our future is wonderful. Our future is glorious. We anticipate the future with great joy. Our prayer should be, "Come, Lord Jesus! Return to us! Give us a new resurrection body! Bring your beautiful kingdom of peace!" Please keep this in mind. Because, the Great Tribulation is a time of unthinkable evil, many people feel afraid and puzzled about the future. This is not how the Lord wants you to feel. The future will be beautiful. We will see the Lord and receive a new body. We will never die!

---

[26] I like to imagine what could be. I do not see any harm in this. However, I will never teach my imaginations. I like the verse that says, "Do not go beyond what is written" (1Corinthians 4:6 NIV). It is very important to draw a line between what is taught in God's word and what we think the future might look like. Be honest and humble and stay with God's word.

The Great Tribulation

The Great Tribulation lasts for seven years and is the greatest time of trouble and distress the world has ever known. It gets its name from an expression found in the Bible that means the time of great trouble. The prophet Daniel was the first to mention it. He wrote,

> And there shall be a time of trouble, such as never has been since there was a nation till that time (Daniel 12:1 ESV).

Jesus also talked about the Great Tribulation in the Gospels. He said,

> For then there will be great tribulation, such as has not been from the beginning of the world until now, no, and never will be. And if those days had not been cut short, no human being would be saved (Matthew 24:21,22 ESV).

The book of Revelation also mentions the Great Tribulation.

> These are the ones who died in the great tribulation. They have washed their robes in the blood of the Lamb and made them white (Revelation 7:14 NLT).

Both Daniel and Jesus say that the time of trouble will be unparalleled in history. There has never been a time like this Great Tribulation and there will never again be a time like it. Jesus' words above are remarkable. He said that if the Great Tribulation was not stopped, no human being would survive. Think about that for a moment. It will be a season of such major, global turmoil that it cannot be compared to any other in world history.

The Great Tribulation lasts for seven years. We learn this from a number of Bible passages. The first is in Daniel 9:25–27 and was written around 530 years before Jesus came to earth. In this text, Daniel prophesied that 483 years would pass between the time that the Jews would return from Babylon until the Messiah would be crucified. Then, Daniel prophesied that there would be another seven–year period of time in the future. It would be a time of war, desolation, of a peace treaty between Israel and the surrounding nations and of someone who would stop all worship in Israel. Other texts that mention the seven–year period of time are Daniel 12:7,11,12; Revelation 11:2,3; 12:6,14; 13:5.[27]

Some people have asked if the Great Tribulation has already begun? The answer is no. We live in a time that Jesus called the "birth pains" (Matthew 24:8). The birth pains mean that we are living in the times leading up to the Great Tribulation. Like birth pains that precede the birth of a child, we live in times of increasing global stress. We can see the signs of the times. We see the wars, disease and famines. We see that God has returned the Jewish people to their land. We see the Good News reaching the ends of the earth. These are signs that the labor pains are beginning, but the Great Tribulation has not yet started. It is close, but we do not live in the Great Tribulation.

The Antichrist

During the Great Tribulation, the nations of the world will become more infuriated with the Jewish people to the point that they will surround Israel in an attempt to annihilate the nation. There will be a man called the antichrist who arises with great power. The name antichrist means a counterfeit messiah. Just like counterfeit money is used to deceive the public into thinking

---

[27] The seven years is broken up into various month and day combinations. For example, 3 ½ years + 3 ½ years, 42 months + 42 months, 1260 days or "times, time and half a time," etc.

it is real money, he will be an imposter messiah who will dupe the world into following him. He will be empowered by Satan (Revelation 13:2), will perform miracles (2 Thessalonians 2:9; Revelation 13:13) and will lead a massive persecution against those who believe in Jesus the Messiah (Revelation 13:5-8). He will be the head of a global economic system that requires his mark in order to trade or make daily financial transactions (Revelation 3:16-17). He will build an idol that looks like himself and place it in the Jewish temple, expecting people to worship it (2 Thessalonians 2:4). The list could go on. But, I want you to see that this person called the antichrist is a central character during this time.[28]

Israel

During the Great Tribulation, the land of Israel will become the center stage of a global drama and the nation of Israel will become the main character in biblical prophecy. We already see that the nation has returned to their land. But, at some point in the near future, we should expect to see Israel constructing a temple. The temple will be used as leverage in a peace agreement between Israel and its neighboring nations (Daniel 9:26-27). It only makes sense that the Jews will be able to build a temple. Think about it. They are the only people on earth who do not have a place to worship their God. Everyone else has churches, temples and mosques. But the Israeli's do not have a temple. They have synagogues. But the temple is their place of worship, not synagogues. Israel will enjoy 3 1/2 years of peace. But after the peace treaty is broken, there will be 3 1/2 years of turmoil for Israel. It is during this time that the antichrist will enter the temple in Israel and set up the idol, as mentioned earlier.

---

[28] He is also called the Man of Lawlessness in 2 Thessalonians 2:3 and the Beast in Revelation 13:1–10; 20:4,10).

Not only is Israel center stage for the antichrist's self–absorbed display, but the nation will become increasingly under fire as death to Israel chants reach fever pitch. As I write, hatred for Israel is on the rise. But the Old Testament prophets, especially Ezekiel 37–39 and Zechariah 12:3; 14:2, tell us how this will culminate with all the nations of the world gathering for war against Israel. Ezekiel gives us the names of several countries, some of whom we know – Russia, Iran, Ethiopia and Libya (Ezekiel 38:2–5).

(3) The Return of the Messiah

The Great Tribulation will end when Jesus the Messiah returns from the sky with great power and glory. As the seven years of trouble reaches an end, all the nations of the world will assemble their armies together and will march against Israel (Zechariah 12:3;14:2). The Lord Jesus will descend from heaven and will defeat the antichrist and all the armies that are attempting to destroy Israel (2 Thessalonians 2:8). The seven years of trouble starts off a bit difficult, experiences some relative peace, only to be followed by an escalation into mayhem like the world has never seen. The Great Tribulation is not the end of the world. All of this is leading somewhere, to the coming of Jesus the Messiah as the King of Kings. When He returns from the sky and defeats the antichrist, He will set up His Kingdom of peace.

(4) The Millennium – Messianic Age of 1000 Years

This seven–year time of the world's greatest trouble will be followed by 1000 years of the world's greatest peace. The Millennium is not a make believe land of utopia for optimistic hopefuls. The Millennium is a time promised through the prophets of Israel to the Jewish nation. It is a time when their Messiah will be on the earth for 1000 years (Revelation 20:2–6), ruling from Jerusalem over all the nations. We who believe in Him, will rule as kings with Jesus in His Messianic kingdom.

The Messiah Returns in Power

Let me list several truths about the millennium. First, the Bible says that Jesus the Messiah will return from the sky to the Mount of Olives (Zechariah 14:4). It was from this location that Jesus ascended into heaven (Acts 1:12). When Jesus' feet touch the Mount of Olives the mountain will split into two parts (Zechariah 14:4), every island will sink into the sea, every mountain will be leveled (Revelation 16:20) and every city of the earth will fall flat with a great earthquake (Revelation 16:18–20).

When Jesus the Messiah returns to earth to be a King, it will not be a small, quiet event. When Jesus came to earth to suffer for our sins, His arrival was quiet. He was born in a barn to humble parents. He lived in obscurity for 30 years. During His life on earth, He allowed people to misunderstand who He was. In fact, in the assessment of Jesus' enemies, He died on the cross as a loser, a loner and another crazy individual who falsely claimed to be the Messiah. But, when Jesus returns to earth as a king, it will not be a quiet event. There will be no mistake in anyone's mind that He is the King of glory. Everyone will see Him. Jesus Himself said,

> Then if anyone tells you, "Look, here is the Messiah," or "There he is," don't believe it . . . So if someone tells you, "Look, the Messiah is out in the desert," don't bother to go and look. Or, "Look, he is hiding here," don't believe it! For as the lightning flashes in the east and shines to the west, so it will be when the Son of Man comes (Matthew 24:23,26,27).

Look! He comes with the clouds of heaven. And everyone will see him, even those who pierced him. And all the nations of the world will mourn for him. Yes! Amen! (Revelation 1:7; Zechariah 12:10).

Satan Bound

Since the garden of Eden, Satan has been free to roam, to cause chaos, to tempt people, to possess individuals and to create deception. I believe that without Satan's help, we as people have great potential for evil. But, we are not alone. We have an unwanted companion. Satan has been alongside every temptation, urging people to do wrong. In the Great Tribulation God gives him great liberty to exercise his full power. Satan even fills the antichrist with the ability to do false miracles. So, we must be very cautious. We must never forget that Satan and his demons are very active in this world at all times. But during the millennium, he will be imprisoned, no longer free to meander.

It would be difficult to imagine a world without Satan and without his demons, because it is all we know. But the Bible tells us that Satan will be bound up and locked away for 1000 years (Revelation 20:1–3). He will no longer be free to roam the earth, to instigate trouble, to tempt people to do evil and to stir rebellion against Jesus. As a result, the 1000 years of the millennium will be a time of true peace.

Change in Topography and Weather

The Bible tells us that there will be a number of changes in the earth's topography and weather. Jerusalem will be elevated to become the highest mountain in all of Israel and the whole earth will be fertile (Zechariah 14:10; Isaiah 2:2; Micah 4:1). A river will flow from Jerusalem to the Mediterranean and Dead Seas (Zechariah 14:8). There will be no frost (Zechariah 14:6).

Change in Animal Kingdom

There will be changes in the temperament and diet of animals. The Bible says that the leopard will lie down with the baby goat. The wolf will live together with the lamb. The calf and the yearling will be safe with the lion. The cattle will graze with the bear. The baby will play near the cobra's hole and not be bitten (Isaiah 11:6–8; 65:25). Imagine this. Today's carnivorous species will become vegetarian. As a result, herbivores will feel relaxed to graze side by side with what were previously their predators. This is a pleasant picture for those of us who cringe at the sight of a lion hunting down and eating a gazelle. And what responsible parent would let their child anywhere near the cobra's nest? The cobra's hole is home to baby cobras and a jealous mama cobra. But, in the millennium an innocent and vulnerable child will safely play near a cobra without the possibility of being harmed. Spend a little time imagining what this could potentially be saying. Does this mean no more dog bites? No more bee stings? No more mosquito bites?

Change in Human Lifespan

There will also be an increase in the human lifespan. During the Millennium, you and I will live in our resurrection bodies and will never die. But the people who make it through the Great Tribulation will repopulate the earth for 1000 years. About them, the Bible says that if someone lives to be 100 years old, people will think the person died as a youth (Isaiah 65:20). In England, if you live to be 100 years old, the Queen will send you a card on your birthday to congratulate you. Living that long is thought to be a major accomplishment, a sign that you are blessed with good health. But, in the millennium, if you only live to be 100 years old, people will consider you to be cursed and to have died as a child. Some have suggested that the human lifespan will be like the days before the flood, when people lived into their 900s.

The Messiah a Warrior

The Bible also tells us that the Messiah will be a mighty warrior. It says that He will rule the earth with a rod of iron (Psalm 2:9). He will warn any nation that plots against Him to overthrow his kingly power (Psalm 2:1–6). In fact, the nations will stand embarrassed at their feebleness in contrast to His strength (Micah 7:16). A plague and panic will strike those who fought against the Messiah (Zechariah 14:12) and with the breath of His mouth, He will destroy the wicked (Isaiah 11:4).

The Messiah a King and Prince of Peace

The Bible also tells us that the Messiah will be a king whose kingdom will be centered in Jerusalem. The Messiah's name will be Prince of Peace and, under His global leadership, the world will experience worldwide peace (Isaiah 9:6,7). Weapons of war will be recycled into farming equipment because there will be no more war or war training exercises (Isaiah 2:4, Micah 4:3). The Messiah will settle international disputes (Isaiah 2:4; Micah 4:3). He will make fair decisions for the exploited and give justice to the poor (Isaiah 11:4). He will rule as a king on David's throne over David's kingdom and will establish worldwide justice and righteousness (Isaiah 9:7). Never again will Jerusalem be destroyed. It will be perfectly secure (Zechariah 14:11).

The Messiah Worshipped

The Messiah will be worshipped. Worshipping the Messiah is a strong statement that proves He is God. After all, only God is worshipped. He will be a teacher, giving the word of the Lord and year after year all the nations will go to Jerusalem to worship Him (Isaiah 2:2,3). He will teach from the temple in Jerusalem (Isaiah 2:3). Not only will all nations make an annual pilgrimage to Jerusalem to worship *"the Lord the King Almighty,"* but they will also celebrate the Feast of Tabernacles (Zechariah 14:16).[29] The Lord will withhold rain and send plagues on the nations that refuse to make their way to Jerusalem for the pilgrimage of worship (Zechariah 14:17–19). There will be a new temple built during the millennium as a place to worship (Zechariah 6:12,13; Isaiah 2:2,3; Ezekiel 40–44).

The Millennium Ends

Sadly, the 1000 years of peace will come to an end. Satan, who was bound, will be released from his prison. He will go to the nations and stir them in rebellion against the Lord and lead them into a great battle against the Messiah. Satan will finally be defeated and then be cast off into the lake of fire and sulfur. There, he will burn forever and ever. This is his final destiny (Revelation 20:3,7–10).

(5) The Final Judgment

Once the Millennium has ended, the Bible tells us that every person who ever lived will be raised to life (Revelation 20:13). It says that there will be a large throne and a final judgment will take place before this throne. The Bible teaches that there are two resurrections (Revelation 20:5–6). The first resurrection is the one we will participate in and it takes place before the millennium, when the Lord Jesus returns in the skies. The second resurrection takes place after the millennium. Those who are raised to life in the second resurrection will be brought before the throne and judged. At this final judgment, a set of books will be opened (Revelation 20:12). The first books are a record of every thought, word and action of every person (Revelation 20:13). Remember, God expects that each person lives a faultless life. Not one sin is permitted. You must be perfect. So,

---

[29] The Feast of Tabernacles is also called the Feast of Booths.

as the record is read and every thought, word and action is made public, how long do you think it would take before one sin is found? Once the first sin is found, the person becomes guilty, is disqualified from entering heaven and worthy of condemnation.

The Bible says that another book is opened. It is called the book of life (Revelation 20:12). The Bible says, *"Anyone whose name who was not found recorded in the book of life was thrown into the lake of fire"* (Revelation 20:15). This judgment is final. There will not be another opportunity for people to choose whether or not they believe in the Messiah. The opportunity to believe is only offered today. Is your name written in the book of Life?

This scene leaves a very mixed feeling in my heart. On one hand you have the beautiful assurance given to those who believe. Because they believed in the Messiah's sacrifice to pay for their sin, their names were written in the book of life and they were rescued from the lake of fire and an eternal destiny of torturous suffering. They did not enter heaven because of their own good works. They entered because they received the gift of God, which is eternal life in Jesus (Ephesians 2:8,9). For those of us who believe in Jesus, we should be the most grateful people on earth. We should meditate on the bliss that will never be taken away from us. Our eternity is beautiful.

On the other hand, there is a very sad ending for millions of people. It is final. There is not a second chance to change their mind. There will not be a weekend to get away from the torment. There will be no more hope, no escape. The average lifespan is only 70 or 80 years, so how can we possibly understand eternity? What a sad, eternal ending for so many people. Jesus taught that hell is a fire, a place of outer darkness, of weeping, pain and anguish that causes people to grind their teeth (Matthew 8:12, 22:13; 25:30). He also spoke about a fire that burned forever, prepared for the devil and his angels and shared by people who are not saved (Matthew 25:41, Luke 16:24,28). This is so unimaginably horrible that it is difficult to think about.

(6) New Heavens and Earth

After this judgement, the Bible tells us that God will burn up the present heavens and earth (2 Peter 3:7,10,12). The fire described in these Bible verses is so intense that it melts even the elements that make up all substances. There will be nothing remaining of the earth, the sky and I would assume that this includes deepest, outer space. Next, from nothing, God will create a new heaven and a new earth (2 Peter 3:13; Revelation 21:1). This is a home of perfection and righteousness. This is our eternal home and it will never pass away. In the new heaven and earth, there will be no more sin, no more death, no more sorrow and no more Satan. We will live forever in new resurrection bodies in a place of eternal bliss. I want to mention a few Bible verses to encourage you with some of the beauty of what we will experience.

> Look, God's home is now among his people! He will live with them, and they will be his people. God himself will be with them. He will wipe every tear from their eyes, and there will be no more death or sorrow or crying or pain. All these things are gone forever (Revelation 21:3,4 NLT).

Isn't this incredible. God wants to take a moment with every hurting person to dry their tears and comfort their misery. Then he will remove all misery, not forgetting the greatest source of misery, death. Can you imagine, no more death? And that's not all. There is a spring where the water gives life. And notice, it is free. It is a reminder throughout all eternity that eternal life does not cost us a penny. It has been given to us as a free gift.

> To all who are thirsty I will give freely from the springs of the water of life (Revelation 21:6 NLT).

We are reminded that all evil and sin is banned forever.

But cowards, unbelievers, the corrupt, murderers, the immoral, those who practice witchcraft, idol worshipers, and all liars – their fate is in the fiery lake of burning sulfur. This is the second death (Revelation 21:8).

I have provided only a few glimpses into what is revealed about heaven in Revelation 21 and 22. We also read about all believers being presented to the Messiah as a bride, a city with gates of pearls, walls of precious stones and streets of pure gold. It is well worth your time to slowly read through this sneak preview of eternity and meditate on how wonderful our future will be.

CONCLUSION

I am sure that this chapter has raised more questions than it has answered. Volumes of books have been published and countless hours of video teachings have been produced that take a much deeper look at what I have covered. As I stated earlier, my intention is to give you a skeletal framework and a brief timeline of the events that are nearer to us with every day that passes.

Be Warned

As you study the future, please avoid arguing over trivial and debatable details and keep in mind that the main aim of prophecy is to warn and to encourage. For me, it is not the confusing prophetic statements that are a problem. It is the clear and easily understood statements that are difficult. The warnings are so clear that they strike the fear of God in my heart and make me repent of anything that hinders my relationship with God. This verse summarizes how I feel.

Therefore, since we are surrounded by such a huge crowd of witnesses to the life of faith, let us strip off every weight that slows us down, especially the sin that so easily trips us up. And let us run with endurance the race God has set before us. We do this by keeping our eyes on Jesus, the champion who initiates and perfects our faith (Hebrews 12:1,2).

Be Encouraged

Just as important, the other goal of prophecy is to encourage us. The Bible says that we are given blessings upon blessings. What do I mean? To start, the Bible says that every believer is already blessed with eternal, spiritual blessings.

> Praise be to the God and Father of our Lord Jesus Christ, who has blessed us in the heavenly realms with every spiritual blessing in Christ (Ephesians 1:3 NIV).

Somehow, although God has already blessed us with every eternal and spiritual blessing, He adds on further rewards for the works we have done. How many small deeds have you done in Jesus name, but have forgotten about them? The Lord has not forgotten. He remembers all your labor for Him and He will reward you. How much have you lost for the Good News? How much have you suffered to bring the Good News to others or to help believers grow in Jesus? Jesus will reward you for your labor when He returns.

> Look I am coming quickly. My reward is with me and I will give to each person according to what they have done (Revelation 22:12 NIV).

Serving Jesus is often a thankless job. Rarely do others understand how much effort you have invested or how much you have sacrificed to accomplish God's work. Don't be surprised at this. Even Jesus healed 10 lepers only to have one return and say thank you (Luke 17:10–19). Since the Lord will reward us for our labor, we should find strength to carry on serving Him. He sees when no one else sees. He remembers, even when we forget. It is the Lord, the Messiah Jesus that we serve.

> So, my dear brothers and sisters, be strong and immovable. Always work enthusiastically for the Lord, for you know that nothing you do for the Lord is ever useless (1 Corinthians 15:58 NLT).

Be Blessed!

Timeline of The Story of the Bible

OLD TESTAMENT		PROPHECIES WRITTEN
Creation – 2000 BC	Chapter 1	**Origins (Genesis 1–11)** **Good** – heaven, earth, human beings, marriage, family, culture **Bad** – sin, death **Solution** – family line of the Messiah who will crush Satan's head **Judgment, Salvation, Faith**
2000 – 1804 BC	Chapter 2	**A Chosen Man: Abraham (Genesis 12–50)** **Promises made to Abraham** – Land, Blessing, Nation, Good News to all Nations, Faith 400 YEARS SILENCE
1525 – 1067 BC	Chapter 3	**A Chosen Nation: Israel (Exodus – Judges)** **The Old Covenant** **The Law** – Ceremonial, Civil, Moral **The Land** – The Lease Agreement **The Land** – Conquered and Portioned
1041 – 971 BC	Chapter 4	**A Chosen Family: David** **(Ruth, 1–2 Samuel, 1 Chronicles)** **Promises made to David** **The Messiah will be the Son of David and the Son of God**
1000 – 430 BC	Chapter 5	**Poetry and Prophecy (28 Books)** **The Prophets and the Land** **The Exile – 70 Years** **Prophecies about (1) Messiah's suffering (2) Good News to all** **Nations (3) The Messiah returning to be a King forever** 400 YEARS SILENCE

NEW TESTAMENT		PROPHECIES FULFILLED
0 – 33	Chapter 6	**Jesus: The Messiah Who Suffered** **(Matthew, Mark, Luke, John)** 10 Claims that Jesus was the Messiah who was predicted to come from the beginning of time.
33 – Present Day	Chapter 7	**The Good News to All Nations** **(Acts and the Letters)** **Acts** – First 30 years of church history **Letters** – 30 more years of church history, Instructions to the Believers, Reaching the Unreached with the Good News
Future 7 Years 1000 Years Eternity	Chapter 8	**Jesus the Messiah is King (Revelation)** **The Great Tribulation** **The Millennium** **The New Heavens and the New Earth**

Final Thoughts

So there you have it. The Story of the Bible, the way Jesus and the apostles told it. Jesus taught the apostles that the entire Bible could be summarized in three prophecies. First, the Messiah would come to earth to suffer and die for sin. Second, the Good News would reach all people of the earth. And third, the Messiah would return to be a king forever. He demonstrated to these men that He was the Messiah and that the time had come for them to bring the blessing of salvation to all nations. The apostles understood what Jesus taught them and they communicated the story to their followers.

New to the Bible?

I know that some of you reading this book, may have never read the Bible or you may have only read a book or two from the Bible. You may have never attended a Bible study or church service. I want you to read the Bible and I hope that this book gives you a way to make sense of it as you read. I also want you to know Jesus and receive the blessing that He has for you. Jesus loves you. He is the Messiah and it is not an accident that you are reading this book. Neither is it a surprise to God. Today is your day to become a part of the prophecy of our time, to receive the blessing of the Messiah Jesus and begin a new life with God.

Familiar to Church and the Bible?

How long have you attended Church? How many sermons, Bible studies and Sunday School classes have you attended? Did you realize that if you have attended church for a number of months or years you may have participated in several hundred meetings?

So, let me ask you a question. After attending all these studies and meetings, were you ever taught the story of the Bible the way that Jesus told it? If not, what have you been taught? If you sat under the apostles' teaching you would be able to take the Old Testament, because that was all they had to work with, and point out the prophecies that foretold the Messiah's suffering, the Good News going to all nations and the Messiah's return as a king.

It is not my intention to oversimplify the Bible and take away from its rich beauty. But as a Bible teacher, it is my responsibility to help you make sense of this ancient book. God inspired the authors to write a permanent record of His story. Then, He gave teachers to illumine the meaning so that believers may be enlightened and empowered with His timeless truth (Ephesians 4:11). My concern is that the big story is missing among the small stories. Or, as the expression says, we miss the forest for the trees. As a result, minor teachings and lesser important themes replace the major teaching and important themes. I want you to see the forest. I want you to understand the main theme.

It is my intention that this book become a valuable resource for your future reference, one that you can return to often. It is my intention to change the way you see the Bible and to make you consider the story as Jesus told it. Today, when the Bible means different things to different people, I believe we need to embrace a simple, accurate interpretation of the whole scripture. We need to remain faithful to the teaching of Jesus and to the teaching of the apostles. We need to understand the story of the Bible the way Jesus and the apostles told it and devote ourselves to it.

All the believers devoted themselves to the apostles' teaching (Acts 2:42 NLT).

Note on Scholarship

Having published and presented academic work, I realize some readers might be expecting a note on the scholarship of this book. And admittedly, an abridged synopsis like this will, by necessity, build upon numerous methodological and theoretical assumptions, which I would like to very quickly address.

First, my intended audience is the general reading public. Consequently, I have deliberately avoided specialist, academic language, cataloguing of authors and their works and discursive arguments that alienate the reader by detracting from the aim of presenting a brief, simplified, comprehensive and cohesive story of the Bible. In an attempt to totalize the macro or grand narrative of the Bible, I do not want to undervalue the complicated and multifaceted nature of biblical, theological or literary studies. I have spent years reading other's works and reflecting upon the Bible's narrative for the purpose of searching out my own assumptions on how I assemble the story. This book and its accompanying video series have emerged from time spent with people, trying to answer their questions, to summarize and simplify, not to complicate.

Second, all dates are based on those commonly accepted among conservative scholars, taking into consideration their disparate opinions. In some cases, the dates used for authorship, lifetime of characters and major biblical events are approximated. When I have used approximated dates, they are accurately represented. Instead of representing the entire lifespan of a character on a timeline, I have chosen a date that falls within their lifetime. For example, I state that Abraham lived 4000 years ago and not his entire lifespan. Why? I want readers to remember the dates that characters lived and events took place. I have discovered that memory is better facilitated by uncomplicated and uncluttered timelines, charts and maps. However, precision has not been compromised for simplicity sake.

I am aware that the volumes of new archaeological research published each year contribute to the ongoing comparative analysis of the biblical account of history with concurrent historical events as recorded in extra–biblical sources. This keeps the discussion on the dates of biblical authorship and the dating of biblical characters and events from stagnating. I would argue that the fluid nature of the discussion has done more to bolster than to undermine the historicity of the biblical account and to reaffirm its credibility than to untether it from reality and condemn it to the dustbin. The Bible remains a credible and reliable source for historiographers.

Third, both within and outside the Christian community, thoughtful arguments on the origins and age of the earth, the origins and age of humanity and not a few popular and scholarly theories of people migration have been forwarded. Some of these theories assimilate the biblical record, others do not and others still seek to discredit it. While I do my best to keep abreast of current studies on origins and ancient people migration, the purpose of this book has been to construct the grand narrative of the Bible and not deviate into various arguments for origins, age and migration.

Fourth, I have studied extensively on the three, primary eschatological views and the sub variations of each. While I am decidedly premillennial, I respect the thoughtful scholarship of the other two views and I have attempted to be tactful in presenting premillennialism.

In summary, this book is undergirded by years of careful scholarship that has taken place in dialogue with an extremely diverse group of people. It is an attempt to bridge a gap between the complexities of scholarly study and the simplicity that most people are searching for and to communicate the Bible's grand narrative as presented through a Lukan optic. It is written in an uncomplicated style that best serves the reading public.

Made in the USA
Lexington, KY
20 September 2016